"WALK TOGETHER CHILDREN AND DON'T GET WEARY"

A Model For Conflict Resolution For Local Congregations In The Church Of God In Christ, Inc.

BY

KEITH C. BRADDY

books

1st. Edition, 2023 - São Paulo, Brazil

Published by UPBooks
A division of Casa Publicadora Bereana Ltda ME
São Paulo, Brazil

Rua Agostinho de Faria, 488 - Cidade Líder
São Paulo, SP - Brazil 08280-100

Printed in Brazil

Walk Together Children and Don't Get Weary
A Model For Conflict Resolution For Local Congregations In The Church Of God In Christ, Inc.

Editor	*Eneas Francisco*
Layout	*BFK Brazil*
Cover design	*Cesar F. Oliveira*
Illustration	*City Church Gathering*
	Artist Unknown

Unless otherwise noted, all scriptures are from the New King James Version of the Bible.

ISBN: 978-65-85258-33-3

DEDICATION

To the blessed memory of my late father:

James Braddy, Sr., (1939–2012)

who gave me a love for learning and taught me the value of getting an education; and my late pastor and spiritual father:

the Right Reverend James Henry Gaylord, D.D.

(1935–2020), the Fourth Jurisdictional Prelate in Succession of the Historic Church of God in Christ, Inc., Eastern New York First Ecclesiastical Jurisdiction and the beloved pastor of the Kelly Temple Church of God in Christ (New York, NY in the Village of Harlem).

He is remembered for faithfulness to his episcopal and pastoral charges and his warm personality, which was the product of his North Carolinian origins. Bishop Gaylord consistently reminded the saints to "keep the unity of the Spirit in the bond of peace" (Ephesians 4:3). Bishop Gaylord's life was tragically cut down by the deadly COVID-19 virus, but his example and Christian witness continue to stand tall as we all await that glorious day, when the "dead in Christ will rise first" and "we who are alive and remain shall be caught up together with them in the clouds to meet the Lord in the air. And thus, we shall always be with the Lord" (I Thessalonians 4:16-17).

AFRICAN AMERICAN SPIRITUAL:

"Walk together, children, don't you get weary,
Walk together, children, don't get weary,
Walk together, children, don't get weary,
There's a great camp meeting in the Promised Land.

Pray together, children, don't you get weary,
Pray together, children, don't get weary,
Walk together, children, don't get weary,
There's a great camp meeting in the Promised Land.

Sing together, children, don't you get weary,
Pray together, children, don't you get weary,
Walk together, children, don't get weary,
There's a great camp meeting in the Promised Land.

Work together, children, don't you get weary,
Work together, children, don't you get weary,
Work together, children, don't you get weary,
There's a great camp meeting in the Promised Land."

ACKNOWLEDGEMENTS

This book is my dissertation that I wrote as a doctoral student at Erskine Theological Seminary that I have modified for the benefit of the saints of the Church of God in Christ, Inc., and other Christians in general who may find it useful. It has always been my desire to be a scholar for the church by providing practical tools that it can use, rather than merely being a scholar in the church. I hope that I have achieved this goal by God's grace.

I would like to thank Dr. Lloyd Melton for his guidance and mentorship during the writing of my Doctor of Ministry dissertation from beginning to end. I also would like to thank some sanctified scholars who were prayerful and intellectual dialogue partners and have reviewed this book with a critical eye in the midst of their busy schedules: Bishop Martin Luther Johnson, J.D., Chief Justice of the Church of God in Christ, Inc., Dr. Eric Williams, the Associate Professor of Theology and Black Church Studies at Duke University Divinity School; Dr. Raynard Smith, Professor of Pastoral Psychology at New Brunswick Theological Seminary and leader of COGIC Scholars; Bishop Herbert R. Davis, Director of the Charles Harrison Mason Bible Institutes and founding pastor of Nehemiah Christian Center COGIC of Durham, North Carolina; and Dr. Jonathan Logan, pastor of Antioch Church of God in Christ in Peoria, Arizona. These aforementioned persons' intellectual acumen and subject matter expertise in their respective disciplines made this book stronger, and the fault is all mine if there are any remaining errors or oversights.

Finally, I cannot close any endeavor of life without thanking God for my wife of over two decades, Kamiti, my loving children Xavier and Rylee, and all my extended family who have affirmed and walked with me in the journey of life. I hope they all know that I love and bless God for them.

Moncks Corner, South Carolina
Ordinary Time 2023

TABLE OF CONTENTS

FOREWORD

One of the earliest biblical texts I committed to memory, in addition to and alongside John 3:16 was the call to holiness recorded in Hebrews 12:14. This biblical call to holiness as recorded by the Hebrew writer was invoked nearly every time our community gathered for worship. What fascinated me most in my youth about this text was that inherent within this passage was a clarion call to peace. In a world that was then and is now ravaged by war, famine, dread and despair, the world's great need for peace has remained ever before me. Within this text you now hold, the author provides his readers with a roadmap to a holiness-inflected call to peace within Christian congregational settings.

In this insightful and thought provoking work, *Walk Together Children*, Dr. Keith Christopher Braddy provides a splendid opportunity for pastors, saints and friends of the Church of God in Christ and other church bodies to pause and reflect repentantly upon ecclesial conflicts that so often wreck congregations, kill pastoral imagination and wound weary and unsuspecting souls. Drawing on his experience as a pastor, chaplain and student of theology, Braddy here proposes a conflict resolution model that is biblically inflected, conversant with current theories of organizational behavior and conflict management, and is capacious enough for the Holy Spirit's intervention and guidance in shepherding parishioners through tumultuous times within the lives of their congregations. In a global religious culture where mediocrity often masquerades as faithfulness, the rare opportunity to pause and reflect upon the originating vision that called us forward and that now beckons us to God's future that awaits us, in this regard, Braddy's reflections are timely, poignant and instructive.

Drawing upon conflict resolution models emanating from within the COGIC tradition, beginning with its founder Bishop Charles Harrison Mason, and other sainted mothers and fathers of the pioneering generation, Braddy rightly proposes the significance of prayer and the intervention of the Holy Spirit as essential to the model he advances. This is consistent with theories of conflict resolution that resonate within the Black Church, the Pentecostal movement in general, and the Black Pentecostal tradition, in particular.

Braddy references biblical motifs from various social, cultural, historic and congregational contexts in both the Hebrew scriptures and the New Testament church, spotlighting poignant examples of conflicts and their resolutions. Braddy also finds persuasive precedent for ways in which divergent communities of faith throughout salvation history have dealt with internal organizational conflict. Braddy valiantly affirms the centrality of scripture as an authoritative source for Christian faith and practice, and commends the Scriptures for deliberation in fashioning the church, as a social institution.

As the Church of God in Christ and other Christian denominations sit poised on the eve of a new era of the church's life and ministry, all churches are mandated by the times to reimagine ministry and even what in the future will constitute a faith community. This refashioning of the church's identity and response are critical as its constituents confront the competing pandemics of race, economics, health, violence and untruths. This is particularly urgent as churches seek to speak life and inject hope into a culture marred and disfigured by death, dread, destitution and despair. Braddy reminds us that the manner in which the church addresses conflict in its own house is a measure of its witness and testimony within the world. Braddy reminds us that the church, as Christ's representative within the earth, is called to provide an alternative view of the possibilities God intends for humanity and the world.

In addition to pastors, engaged laity, and students of theology, I highly recommend this text for everyday Christians who long to see the church and the congregation as a place of wholeness and healing. This book will be useful to those desirous of ushering in life affirming cultures and ecologies of peace within our faith communities and world, that the name of Christ in all things might be glorified.

Eric Lewis Williams, Ph.D.
Director, Office of Black Church Studies
Assistant Professor of Theology and Black Church Studies
Duke University School of Divinity
Durham, North Carolina

CHAPTER ONE

WHEN YOUR CHURCH BECOMES FAMOUS THE WRONG WAY

"Don't let his name go down.
Don't let his name go down.
I got to do all I can to hold up that name,
Don't let his name go down."

A historic 102-year-old Williams Temple Church of God in Christ (COGIC) in Houston, Texas was shaken to its core by a bitter church dispute concerning calls for the removal of its pastor—who happened to be among COGIC's episcopacy. Williams Temple membership called for COGIC to remove the pastor from its congregation because he was criminally charged for sexual battery and an allegation of financial misconduct.[1] The conflict of this Houston COGIC congregation raged until the pastor was removed, and was reinstated again by the denomination because of a legal technicality,[2] and it finally ended with the pastor's resignation.[3] Sadly, the pastor's departure came too late to prevent a 75% membership drop of this once-thriving historic COGIC congregation and the tarnishing of the reputation of the COGIC denomination itself.[4]

Another example of destructive church conflict can be seen in the case of the Los Angeles, California Pacific Mt. Olive COGIC congregation whose church conflict erupted and spilled out beyond its Board of Trustees, church membership, Los Angeles community, two California COGIC ecclesiastical jurisdictions, and, ultimately, the denomination itself, even to its highest pinnacles of authority. This Los Angeles COGIC church had many pastoral turnovers that fractured the congregation and its standing in the community throughout its 98-year history, despite having several real estate holdings.[5]

One of the many "pastoral woes" of the Pacific Mt. Olive COGIC came about because of a legal dispute that arose between the Board of Trustees and its former pastor while the church was a member of the Southern California Ecclesiastical Jurisdiction.[6] The point of contention of this Los Angeles congregation was an allegation of the misappropriation of church funds by the former pastor for "personal gain" without the trustees' consent.[7] The Jurisdictional Prelate attempted to intervene in the church conflict to no avail. The feud between Pacific Mt. Olive's trustees and pastor consummated in its pastor's resignation in August 2013.[8] Reportedly, the church was also subsequently dismissed from its ecclesiastical jurisdiction by their bishop so that the staff could find episcopal leadership more to their approval.[9]

Eventually, Pacific Mt. Olive became entangled in a new conflict with the denomination when an elder of another COGIC congregation was allegedly hired as the pastor of Pacific Mt. Olive COGIC contrary to the policy of COGIC. [10] In addition, some of the trustee board members claimed that they were illegally removed from their office incongruent with the Pacific Mount Olive COGIC local church's Bylaws. Finally, there were a disagreement between the denomination and Pacific Mt. Olive COGIC as to which ecclesiastical jurisdiction it was a member after its dismissal from Southern California Ecclesiastical Jurisdiction. What is clear despite the conflicting accounts is that the destructive conflict of Pacific Mt. Olive COGIC divided its congregation, as well as damaged its reputation and that of COGIC through the widespread negative media and social media coverage, so much so that the general counsel of the denomination had to publish a statement on the matter to defend the actions of its leadership.[11]

The Williams Temple and Pacific Mt. Olive COGIC attest to the fact that COGIC has not been spared the reality of destructive congregational conflicts within its local churches—like any other denomination—despite its reputation for jubilant worship and its theological emphasis on sanctification and supernatural spiritual gifts among its members. The sad reality is that the most gruesome sins that break sacred bonds, assassinate the character of other Christians, and impede a local church from carrying out its sacred mission are done by those who call themselves "saints."[12]

Also, the Williams Temple and Pacific Mt. Olive COGIC are two classic examples of how church conflicts can germinate, grow, and lay waste to the church, denomination, and people of God. Put another way, these two models of church conflict—and there are many more—demonstrate how you can make your congregation famous—or more accurately infamous—when church conflict is not understood, ecclesiastical boundaries are not defined, and integrity is not followed in all manner of conduct in God's church. In fact, when church conflict occurs—as it did in Williams Temple and Pacific Mt. Olive—pastors and church members become psychologically and spiritually weary of the very community—or lack thereof—that they are called to be a part of. Indeed, the devastating disputes that happen within buildings adorned with stained glass make it difficult to walk, sing, pray, and work together as children of God in God's kingdom.

Common Approaches to Church Conflict

COGIC pastors and church leaders who face destructive congregational conflict within their churches usually respond in two common ways. First, some COGIC pastors who face destructive conflict within their churches simply surrender to it. This occurs whenever church leaders—particularly pastors—choose to deny the existence of destructive conflict within their congregation; alternatively, by quietly ignoring it, they are hoping that it will disappear on its own. Second, other COGIC pastors deal successfully with destructive congregational conflict by the trial-and-error method of conflict resolution.

These two typical approaches to conflict resolution used in COGIC churches are problematic for two reasons. On the one hand, surrendering to conflict by denying and/or avoiding it is usually futile. Those who are astute as to the dynamics of church conflict know that bad news—in the case of church conflict—does not usually get better over time. Indeed, there are times when conflict avoidance can be a wise approach, but oftentimes, it is little more than conflict cowardice. Hare notes that, regarding the strategy of conflict avoidance to unhealthy church conflict, "more often than not it only postpones the inevitable and usually makes things worse" within a congregation.[13] On the other, the trial-and-error approach is not a desirable method of dealing with church conflict in COGIC because it can be very painful. A solution to the church conflict arbitrarily discovered by the trial-and-error process typically leaves—both pastors and congregations—spiritually shaken and psychologically damaged even after the season of church conflict has passed. Most COGIC pastors, as well as many bishops and district superintendents if they were honest, are not knowledgeable in how to deal effectively with destructive congregational conflict that may erupt within their churches—even if they are seminary trained—which is still a very small minority of the presbytery of the denomination. In addition, the COGIC denomination has no official resource to help guide and/or train its pastors in how to navigate through the vortex of church conflict, even though it is the most common ecclesiastical reality that will test their pastoral leadership.

The rationale for this book emerged out of a practical need to provide a solution that resolves the destructive church conflict that I encountered in my last pastoral charge. Although I was adequately prepared to minister to my church members with exegetical, theological, and homiletical prowess, I now know that I was not equipped to deal with the destructive, congregational conflict that erupted at the beginning of my pastoral tenure during an economic recession.[14] I sought counsel from my jurisdictional leadership in those turbulent times so that I could get their insights into how to deal with my church conflict. However, I was shocked to discover that their advice to me was mostly to acquiesce to the conflict and just wait for my congregational antagonists to die or leave. Far worse, I painfully discovered that my congregational antagonists frequently manipulated and/or made complicit to my harm the very jurisdictional leaders whom I trusted for help. Unfortunately, the actions of my jurisdictional leaders affirm an observation made by Hare regarding denominational leaders and church conflict that I wish I would have known in my past experiences. He said, "Denominations differ greatly in the resources they can provide to help congregations in conflict. Some are great, but others may lack knowledge and skill and may even make things worse."[15]

My own existential trauma of church conflict in a congregation that I led for almost a decade made clear that COGIC had no clear means of helping its pastors with this perplexing problem. It also made clear that even the most senior of pastors in my former jurisdictional hierarchy lacked accurate knowledge on how to deal with destructive congregational conflict. Unfortunately, this lack of knowledge by my ecclesiastical leadership made the church conflict that I experienced worse.

Therefore, I know from painful experience that COGIC jurisdictional leaders, pastors, and congregations desperately need a denominational resource to effectively deal with destructive church conflict that would give them the confidence to face—rather than evade—the ecclesiastical turmoil in their midst. The denomination in general—and COGIC congregations in particular—requires an effective tool that is rooted in research, highly skilled in mediation, and congruent with its own theological identity, which would allow pastors and congregations to use proven methods of conflict resolution instead of painful, unsystematic trial-and-error approaches that hope for the best but usually get the worst results. This book will address this need by proposing the creation of a COGIC conflict resolution team, hereafter called the CCRT.

In my book, I will argue that the primary reason for advocating for a CCRT in dealing with congregational conflict within the COGIC is twofold. On the one hand, a CCRT is a biblical approach to conflict resolution and mediation. This is the case because the Scriptures frequently command the participation and intervention of more than just the disputing parties in a conflict. This is the case because more than just the conflicting parties' involvement is usually necessary to achieve true reconciliation because our sinful nature resists the reconciliation that people claim to seek. On the other, this book proposes the use of CCRT in a fractured COGIC congregation because a team of men and women with specific skill sets should allow a particular congregational dispute to be viewed with a holistic lens that can foster successful mediation and resolution.

Moreover, this book will make its case for a CCRT in four subsequent chapters. Chapter II will explain the roots of church conflict and what congregational stressors tend to cause its eruption. Chapter III will focus on the biblical foundation for a CCRT and why it is appropriate for use within a church. Chapter IV will focus on who should constitute the CCRT and why each member of this CCRT is important to seeing a particular dispute within a congregation holistically. Chapter V will provide a conclusion on this research topic.

CHAPTER ONE

[1] Lacy Individually Represented as Williams Temple Church of God in Christ Court of Appeals Texas, Fourteenth District, Houston (March 30, 2004); Bruce Nolan, "Pentecostal Bishop Charles Brown Booked with Sexual Battery," *The Times-Picayune*, September 21, 2011, https://www.nola.com/news/crime_police/article_0242250c-fff9-5d6b-a5b1-d6d3f1c5e0a4.html.

[2] The legal technicality caused the Presidium of the COGIC to reinstate Bishop Charles Brown because the statute of limitation for sexual battery in the state of Louisiana had expired; thus, the charges were dropped against the pastor of Williams Temple COGIC; John Simerson, "Sex Charge against a Pentecostal Bishop Was Filed Too Late, Judge Says," *The Times-Picayune,* March 3, 2012, https://www.nola.com/news/crime_police/article_40aed0ae-4e4a-5737-bf93-62474a569dd1.html; and Bruce Nolan, "COGIC Reinstates Bishop after Criminal Case Is Dropped," *The Washington Post,* March 7, 2012, https://www.washingtonpost.com/national/on-faith/cogic-reinstates-bishop-after-criminal-charges-dropped/2012/03/07/gIQAjUfGxR_story.html. Bishop Charles Brown was not reinstated by the General Board (the Presidium) to the Williams Temple COGIC because he was found to be innocent of the allegations made against him, which would have tarnished his reputation.

[3] Nolan, "COGIC Reinstates Bishop"; and Simerson, "Sex Charge against a Pentecostal Bishop."

[4] COGIC Abuse Watch, 'Numerous Assault Complaints Filed against National Trustee Cari Barnes," July 3, 2014, https://cogicabusewatch.wordpress.com/tag/williams-temple/.

[5] Ulesses C. Henderson Jr., Esq., "Statement on Pacific Mount Olive Church of God in Christ," Office of the General Counsel, http://cogicjustice.net/wp-content/uploads/2016/11/2016-11-03-Statement-

on-Mount-Olive-COGIC.pdf.

[6] Ibid., 2.

[7] Ibid., X.

[8] Ibid., 1.

[9] Ibid., 2.

[10] The General Counsel of COGIC asserts that Elder Joyner was never appointed by a jurisdictional prelate as required by the COGIC Constitution for a pastoral appointment to be valid but was made "the interim pastor" in a "special meeting" by the Board of Trustees of Pacific Mt. Olive (cf. Ibid., 2). These reported actions of the Board of Trustees made Elder Joyner's status as pastor illegitimate and void in the eyes of the denomination.

[11] Ibid., 1.

[12] The term "saint" used in COGIC does affirm the general Protestant notion that all Christians are holy because of their justification in a general sense and, as such, are saints. However, COGIC's use of the term has an even deeper theological and social meaning, as noted by historian Anthea Butler. She explained that the term "saint" was used in Holiness-Pentecostalism and COGIC, in particular, to refer to a person who "has made a personal commitment to living a sanctified life": As such, it was a boundary designation that separated church members from those who were considered outsiders. The term "saint" was also "a form of address" that affirmed the personhood of African American Christians in the days of intense racism when overt racism was the most intense; cf.; Anthea D. Butler, *Women in the Church of God in Christ: Making a Sanctified World* (Chapel Hill: The University of North Carolina Press, 2007), 66. This was the case because this simple designation was "particularly important at a time when African-Americans were often called 'Boy', 'Mammy', or other derogatory, generic terms rather than their given names" (cf. Ibid., 66).

[13] Michael Hare, *When Church Conflict Happens: A Proven Process for Resolving Unhealthy Disagreements and Embracing Healthy Ones* (Chicago: Moody Publishers, 2019), 34.

[14] Many theological seminaries are gifted at training their students in theology and biblical studies but neglect practical ministry and leadership training other than classes on preaching.

[15] Hare, *When Church Conflict Happens,* 22.

CHAPTER TWO

THE NATURE OF CHURCH CONFLICT

"O Zion what's the matter now?
O Zion what's the matter now?
You don't sing like you used to sing.
What's the matter now?
You don't shout like you used to shout.
What's the matter now?"[1]

A Mature View of Church Conflict

Not all congregational conflicts are evil or lead to institutional destruction. Simply put, "conflict is neutral" because it can be either "good or bad, healthy or unhealthy creative or destructive" as Haugk noted.[2] A healthy church can find itself in conflict—consciously or unconsciously—in the noble attempt to find solutions to new challenges that it faces in the present moment. Indeed, every church captivated by the Great Commission and sincerely concerned about its members and its witness to its community and the world seeks, as Charles Wesley's hymn says, "To serve the present age, our calling to fulfill."[3]

Unfortunately, many Christians—both clergy and laity—

mistakenly equate church health as the absence of tension and/or conflict. Certainly, the Scriptures do place a high value on peace in the local church and exhort Christians to "Make every effort to keep the unity of the Spirit in the bond of peace" (Ephesians 4:3 NIV). However, as Anyabwile and Adams assert, biblical peace in the local church is rooted in ecclesiastical health and not merely because church members get along or work together in activities and/or projects.[4] In fact, these authors argue that sometimes the peace of a congregation must be disturbed to return the church back to health, such as in the case of confronting an unrepentant, morally backslidden member or pastor.[5] They write, "A church can be at peace while false things are sometimes taught, unqualified or disqualified leaders are at the helm, discipline and love are missing, and the church's government is more worldly than biblical. People can get along and even grow in number despite all those things being out of whack. That's because God is gracious."[6] Christian leaders should not strive for peace in itself, but, more importantly, they should seek to lead a healthy church that will automatically produce biblical peace.

Thus, the presence of church conflict is not always a sign that things in a congregation are going wrong. Contrary to this widely held belief, what we may perceive as church conflict can sometimes be the providential stirrings of the Holy Spirit compelling a congregation to envision new vistas of ministry opportunities or free itself from its outdated paradigms that it has clung to for decades and that continue to hinder it from realizing its mission.

Hare affirms this truth when he writes that, "Depending on the underlying issues and how people respond, conflict can actually become a healthy platform for problem-solving and spiritual growth."[7] This should not surprise us because congregational challenges, such as personal ones, oftentimes motivate Christians to become more creative and seek God more frequently and fervently in prayer. Bolman and Deal concur with this truth from a secular standpoint when they write about conflicts and organizations:

> Conflict has benefits as well as its cost: "a tranquil, harmonious organization may very well be apathetic, uncreative, stagnant, inflexible, and unresponsive organization. Conflict challenges the status quo [and] stimulates interest and curiosity. It is the root of personal and social change, creativity, and innovation. Conflict encourages new ideas and approaches to problems, stimulating innovation."

Indeed, it is true that church conflict can be a foe when it mutates into its destructive forms that foster division, bitterness, and hatred, which I will discuss much later. Nevertheless, church conflict can also be an unsuspecting friend to a congregation when its positive consequences are recognized, and its potential destructive tendencies are kept at bay. Surprisingly, when church conflict is viewed from this standpoint, the problem of some local churches is that they have "too little conflict."[8]

On the one hand, the diversity within a local congregation itself can cause church conflict to emerge within local churches in two significant ways. First, the diversity within a local church can cause conflict because of differing understandings about beliefs and the value of various ministries within a congregation. The frequently forgotten fact is that, although the leadership and membership of a congregation are generally committed to shared common goals (e.g., evangelism, discipleship, worship)—at least theoretically—people who sit in pulpits and pews do not think alike about them or always agree on how these common goals should be achieved. In addition, church members and pastors do not value all ministries with the same degree of worth. Congregants may agree that all aspects of ministry have inherent value, but each individual attaches higher or lower degrees of worth to certain ministry elements.[9] This reality explains why certain ministries in congregations receive more or less financial funding in church budgets and others receive more or less staffing and/or volunteers. These varying degrees of worth concerning elements of ministry are influenced by congregational ecology and overall demographics such as race, regional ethos, "generation, economics, class, and education."[10]

Moreover, congregants and clergy may corporately hold to certain confessional beliefs in a general sense that they consider to be "truth," such as a denomination's statement of faith, but hold differences as to what these truths mean in a practical sense. For example, a congregation may unanimously hold to a belief in holiness and sanctification, but individual members may differ as to the application of those beliefs in matters of dress, recreation, and/or ecumenical relationships. This is the case because an individual's "beliefs [always] shape the issue" of what truth is by means of their hermeneutical process, regardless of whether they are conscious of it.[11] Therefore, the inherent diversity of church congregations should make it understandable why perspectives will differ and sometimes clash even in the absence of malice. The mature Christian—both laity and clergy alike—should respect and treasure this diversity within their local congregation and see church conflicts that arise from it as unavoidable but not evil in every circumstance. Since the Church—both universally and locally—is the image of the Trinity, it is called to oneness and not sameness, just as the Trinitarian persons are one and are not the same.[12] Consequently, a faithful local church can have differences within it when it comes to values and practical understandings of truth in creative tensions, and they can still be rooted in Christian charity. Christians who lack the maturity to comprehend the oneness that Christ calls for in the Church—when he fervently prayed "that they may be one" over two millenniums ago—can mutate God's gathered community into the image of a fallen human being at best or a cult at worst (John 17:21 NKJV).

Then again, limited resources in manpower and treasure of a congregation—regardless of its size—can also lead to church conflict. *The Nonprofit Source* reports that only 10-25% of church members in most congregations are tithers and that the contributions of this small minority of church members fluctuate with the state of their economic realities at a particular time.[13] Thus, there is a limit to how much finance a local congregation can raise and spend on a particular task within the church at a given time. In addition, there is a limit to the number of volunteers and/or paid employees who can be dedicated to a specific task or ministry.[14] This limit to the manpower of churches is even more relevant when it is understood that most American churches are not large, which is contrary to the images of mega churches that dominate religious broadcasting. *Christianity Today* reported in a 2019 article that 57% of all churches are 100 members or less and 21% of American churches have 50 members or less.[15] This means that 78% of all American churches have less than 100 members. Moreover, it should be understood that the workforce of congregations is even smaller if we consider that all enrolled members do not volunteer in their local churches. Consequently, because local churches are limited regarding human and financial resources, the people who constitute the leadership and membership of a congregation will have different ideas on how to use the limited resources of finances and manpower, which has the potential to create church conflict "as surely as night follows day."[16]

Finally, basic sociological realities of a congregation can cause conflict to emerge within local churches. The simple fact is that although the people of God constitute a spiritual organism, local congregations are human organizations that are composed of auxiliaries, church boards, clergy, and laity. Consequently, the sociological reality of the local church is that it is a human "organization of coalitions" of persons with particular interest as to the church's identity and operation and their place in it. Burns, Chapman, and Guthrie rightly highlight this fact in their book *The Politics of Ministry*. They write that "all have interest. Our interest usually reflects the way we think the world should function. Interest can be described as deep-seated values, goals, and beliefs. Often, interest sits in the back of our consciousness, strongly yet secretly influencing our opinions and decisions. They steer us like the ruddy of a ship."

As a result, members and leaders in congregations "bargain with other players [auxiliary leaders, church mothers, pastors, affluent members, etc.] to influence goals and decisions that align with their interest." It is important to note that, oftentimes when the word "interest" is mentioned in sacred and secular matters, the negative connotation of self-centeredness is automatically attached to it. Although this is certainly true in many situations—both secular and sacred—it is not always true in all cases involving interest. For example, a person's interest in a local congregation can be to promote a particular ministry/auxiliary (e.g., music ministry) of a local church, even though such a promotion can be at the expense of another ministry (e.g., youth ministry) due to limits upon treasure and manpower that exist in all congregations. Church conflicts can remain manageable when church leaders and members are aware of their interest instead of acting as if they have none. Indeed, it is better to be transparent and state what one's interest is upfront in the matters of the church then to be cloaked in the soiled rags of a pseudo-neutrality that will be discovered to be disingenuous much later.

Church Conflict: The Hard Truth

The previous section showed that church conflict cannot be avoided because of the inherent sociological realities and congregational diversity that exist within any church. Simply put, differences in personalities and perspectives about how to manage limited resources within a congregation will lead to inevitable disagreements, although these disagreements are not—nor do they have to be—always destructive. Moreover, it has been shown that it is possible for church conflict to be an unsuspecting friend that can guide a church from discord to rebranding, which can ultimately consummate into its organizational revitalization. However, all church conflicts are not the same. Sometimes they can be a pernicious foe, occasionally mutating into disputes that are bitter, chaotic, and personal, which can rightly be characterized as un-Christian. Nevertheless, the question we must now consider is this: Can destructive congregational conflict be attributed solely to diversity alone? Does the political frame theory from business and sociology adequately explain why human interest can become so irrational? Is another lens required to comprehend why church disagreements sometimes turn into divisions that break the sacred bonds of fellowship within a congregation?

Many Christians—COGIC and non-COGIC alike—are perplexed as to how destructive congregational conflict could ever exist among those who piously sit upon pews when most do claim to genuinely love God and their fellow believers in Christ. Nevertheless, church members may be confused as to the reason for destructive conflict within their midst, but the Scriptures and the Christian theological tradition are not. Theological anthropology contends that destructive congregational conflict can never be properly understood—let alone resolved—without an accurate understanding of the reality of sin that exists within human beings. Reformation theology —particularly as articulated by Martin Luther—defines Christians as *simul Justus et peccator*. So, even though Christians sing melodious hymns, read sacred text, and don clerical collars and ecclesiastical robes in churches, all of them are fallen human beings prone to error. This means that "all parts of the soul" of the Christian are thoroughly "possessed by sin" as the reformer John Calvin once put it in his famous *Christian Institutes* penned five centuries ago. In fact, the Christian's very "will," which must be used to decide whether to negotiate, compromise, or even listen to other believers attentively and sincerely, "is wicked" outside of the constraining influence of grace. Poirier rightly maintains that "Conflict erupts with all kinds of evil—slander, gossip, blame-shifting, malice, anger, factions, and so on—because there is evil in our [Christian] hearts." These things occur when Christians "walk in their flesh [sinful fallen humanity]" instead of allowing their humanity to be controlled by the loving influence of the Holy

Spirit, which allows them to live in a continued state of genuine repentance (Galatians 5:16-18). This sad truth is a hard reality for most Christians to accept about others, and it is definitely difficult for them to accept about themselves, but the sooner they do, the better for all.

A wide-eyed view of the sinfulness of Christians in church conflicts reminds us of three important truths. On the one hand, just because Christians in the local church are indeed "sanctified in Christ Jesus," their status of positional sanctification should not be misconstrued to mean that they cannot—and/or do not—sin against God and each other after their conversion and baptism in the Holy Spirit (I Corinthians 1:3). Such notions of sanctification are incongruent with the total witness of Scripture or the lived reality of the Christian experience in our denomination or anywhere else. For example, Bishop William Roberts—the first COGIC state overseer of the state of Illinois—became "inflamed and said many things publicly against the Senior Bishop," Charles Harrison Mason in 1947, because he divided the one jurisdiction of the state of Illinois into two. Bishop Roberts was known by all to be a saintly man, and he once served as Bishop Mason's assistant pastor at the historic Temple COGIC in Memphis, Tennessee, prior to his relocation to Chicago, Illinois, at the request of the late Mother Lillian Brooks Coffey. Nevertheless, despite Bishop Robert's status as a sanctified believer, he still sinned by "speaking evil of Bishop Mason" of which he later publicly repented. In another instance in 1948, some leaders within COGIC's Pastor's and Elder's Council accused Bishop Mason of "ex[h]orting too much [sic] dictatorial powers" over the denomination that he founded. Even further, six COGIC pastors, two laypersons, and seven elders initiated a law suit against Bishop Mason and the COGIC denomination. The bill of injunction issued against the denomination in the lawsuit claimed that Bishop Mason was also financially corrupt and that the COGIC General Board was "complicit in Mason's corruption." This lawsuit generated notable negative media coverage for COGIC and its chief apostle at the time where the denomination was accused in the press of being "rotten to the core." In the end, the lawyers for COGIC and the disgruntled parties accepted a compromise "by the request of the attorneys" to settle matters among themselves. When the financial records of the denomination had been thoroughly reviewed, it was shown that Bishop Mason was not financially corrupt, but was owed money by numerous COGIC clergypersons because he had given thousands of dollars out in personal loans. The lawsuit against Mason and the denomination was dropped and leaders of COGIC Pastor's and Elders Council publicly apologized to Mason and the denomination's leadership. Some wanted to expel the disgruntled pastors who were behind the lawsuit, but Mason demanded that those persons be forgiven and restored to full fellowship instead.

These historical examples demonstrate that, unfortunately, church disputes can sometimes make the most pious among us behave ungodly even when we strive not to be so, especially when power, status, influence, and money are intertwined in the dispute.

Gangel and Canine provided a reminder of the nature of church conflicts and people in Christian churches when they wrote, "People in Christian organizations, especially those coming from secular organizations expect utopia [in the church]. However, Christians do not check their old natures at the door when signing contracts or securing employment in a Christian organization."

Consequently, the ancient words of the saintly African prelate Augustine are true for us today when he said, "There are texts of Scripture which seem to me to lay down that no man in this life, free though he be to choose, is ever found without sin." Therefore, the most pious among us must still pray "Forgive us our trespasses" because, "as far as we know," God did not "remove from a man all need for such prayer," as Augustine rightly noted.

On the other hand, the spirituality of a congregation's leadership is the greatest "immune system" to keep the destructive disease of ungodly and bitter conflict at bay. This is the case because a robust Christian spirituality—nurtured by consistent prayer and introspection—gives congregational leaders the ability to restrain their pride and stay focused on their relationship with God and neighbor, as well as the fundamentals of the faith. The entire congregational leadership—and not just the pastor—sets the tone for this vibrant spirituality that seeks to restrain rather than remove church conflict. Steinke writes, "Comparable to the brain's functioning in the body is the functioning of the leaders in the congregation. They are in the position to influence the emotional field [of a church] in far reaching ways."

Finally, a knowledge of the sinfulness of Christians in ecclesiastical disputes should move us all—clergy and laypersons alike—to humility to do some deep and honest soul searching whenever church conflicts arise. The fruit of sincere soul searching of an authentic pious Christian is to consider the possibility that, whenever we are involved in a bitter disagreement within the Church—individually or corporately—it could very well be because of our own sinfulness. This is the case because vice goes beyond immorality. Some Christians are sanctified from addictive substances but are severely bound to an unholy addiction to stubbornness and a selfish will to power that fosters destructive conflict in the house of God. Also, this realization that imperfect Christians constitute the congregation to which we are members should not cause us to withdraw from active participation within that which we are attached in covenant. Indeed, some Christians become disillusioned by the truth that destructive church conflict reveals about their fellow church members and seek to find a congregation that is conflict free and filled with nothing but perfect believers. Such a search among these disillusioned Christians is futile because such a congregation does not exist. The fact of the matter is that "Christian community is not an ideal, but a divine reality," as Dietrich Bonhoeffer wrote decades ago. The Church does not exist because it is perfect, but, to the contrary, it exists because the perfect God called it into being through the womb of the Spirit and sustains it, despite our collective and individual imperfections. The fact that individual congregations are a part of the one holy Church says more about God than our own individual claim to personal holiness.

Congregational Stressors

Destructive congregational conflicts do not occur in a church out of osmosis, but they are usually the consequence of anxious reactions to one or more congregational stressors. Congregational stressors can be defined as incidents and/or events within a life of a church that can cause persons—and possibly the whole congregation—to be filled with anxiety. There are three kinds of congregational stressors that typically trigger anxiety within a local church and make it susceptible to destructive disagreements when not handled properly: congregational change from external and internal causes, professional misconduct that breaches congregational trust, and undefined and/or perceived transgressed boundaries by an individual or individuals related to power in a congregation. These aforementioned congregational stressors are "an effect [that the] people do not like"—(e.g. betrayal, concern for financial survival of the church, a loss or perceived loss of power and/or influence)—in which members and/or clergy become anxious because they believe themselves to be personally threatened by an action of another that has affected them. This perception of being threatened by a congregational stressor causes individuals in the congregation to become reactive, putting them into a Fight or Flight mode that is dominated with emotionally-charged thoughts of self-preservation at any cost. This survival-driven mode of being that is generated by the lower brain is manifested in church fights by impulsive and imprudent words and actions that damage a congregation. This is the case because the part of the brain that instinctively takes over when we feel threated by a congregational stressor is "more thoughtless, more instinctive and automatic." People consumed in congregational conflict tend to focus on "a single cause or culprit" to blame, rather than take a panoramic view of a stressor in light of the congregation and corresponding local church's ecology as a whole. This is understandable when we consider that conscious rational thought originates from the neocortex part of the [upper] brain that is used when we are calm and feel safe; the exact opposite of what we feel in a church fight. Consequently, it takes great spiritual and natural discipline—as well as persistent practice—"to exercise veto power over the instinctive forces of the two lower brains," which motivates us to fight or run in destructive church conflict when we are overtaken in anxiety.

It should be noted that anxious events do not automatically cause destructive conflict within congregations because—as with anything—association does not produce causation. To the contrary, destructive conflict can emerge only when a person—or persons—willingly serves as a host to negativity because "All anxiety needs a host cell, a co-contributor." People enable the virus and/or cancer of destructive conflict to enter a congregation by choosing to become a host and involving themselves in irresponsible behaviors. These irresponsible behaviors alleviate the anxiety of a person within a local church but transfers it to other members within the congregational system by their actions; thus, it weakens the overall health of the church.

The most notorious, irresponsible behavior that frequently contributes to destructive congregational conflict is murmuring. There are four elements of murmuring that should be remembered regarding congregational conflict. First, murmuring can be defined as secretive negative comments about church policy, practices, and/or its leadership—senior or subordinate—that express themselves in "gossip, accusations (blaming/ faultfinding) lies (deception) and triangulation (shifting burdens to others)." Second, murmuring occurs in the shadows of the congregation—either directly or technologically by way of social media—and attempts to masks one's position from those they are in opposition to, while still damaging them with the words they convey. Third, murmuring should be viewed as sinful because it is a form of verbal violence that attacks, calls into question, and/or destroys the integrity of a leader, leaders of a local church, or the very church itself. Moreover, murmuring is sinful communication because it seeks to evade expressing a disagreement with a person or church leadership directly, and it makes us emotionally uncomfortable and vulnerable to possible retaliation when our feelings are disclosed to those in power whom we disagree with. Nevertheless, reconciliation and not our comfort and institutional safety should receive priority in church disputes. Jesus Christ commanded that the Church express our disagreements with other Christians in a direct manner (Matthew 18:15-17).

Steinke rightly notes that when we fail to express our disagreements openly—assuming that we are right—it is "utterly neglectful of the evangelical counsel "to speak the truth in love" (Ephesians 4:15). Christians should take note that the sin that brought judgment to an entire generation of Israelites, which led to their destruction in the wilderness—excluding Joshua and Caleb—was that of murmuring (Numbers 14:1-24; Psalms 106:24-27). Consequently, God's distaste of murmuring should not be ignored by contemporary Christians because the Old Testament was written for our present warning and example and so that we do not duplicate the errors of the ancient people of God in our local congregations (II Corinthians 10:1-12).

Finally, murmuring should never be misconstrued with the principled verbal exchange and/or honorable disagreement. This is the case, because loyal or honorable disagreement is expressed openly, tactfully, and in legitimate forums such as business meetings where a topic is debated and discussed. Moreover, honorable disagreement is problem-oriented rather than "person-oriented" dispute, whereby a person or group's opposition views them as an enemy. When a person honorably disagrees, they discuss their issue directly to a person in which there is disagreement and not through others within the congregation, which produces triangulation. Therefore, the loyal opposition and/or honest disagreement is distinguished from murmuring in that it articulates its concern with "straightforward" language with "no hidden agendas" that sincerely seeks to find a "rational" and "amicable resolution to conflict."

The following looks at some typical congregational stressors:

Congregational Change

All churches are either amid congregational change or that change wills that soon confront it. The simple fact of congregational life is that change can be resisted or even delayed in a local church, but it cannot be stopped. Change comes to a local church when its stability and/or normal course of operations is threatened and/or altered because the congregation's ecology has been amended internally or externally in some way.

There are two common examples of changes in congregational ecology that cause changes in a local church. The first alteration in congregational ecology that can compel change in a local church can emerge from external forces within the community in which a church is located. This could be dismal economic realities within the church's community or region that prevents church members from finding employment, or a job that would give them a living wage. As a result, this external economic reality can lead to church membership decline because congregants may feel forced to relocate from the town, city, or region where their church is to survive and/or thrive. This economic reality can also affect how much revenue the church receives, and how many volunteers it can generate to achieve steps to realize its mission. Finally, dismal economic realities can transform the congregational ecology by altering a local church's demographic. As previously stated, if people cannot thrive where they live and where their church is located, they will eventually move to places where thriving is possible. In most cases, this means that youth and young adults are the key demographic in the local church that decreases from this ecological shift. This trend strains the congregation because "change in one part [of the congregation] produces change in another part" of the church.[17] A church may find it difficult to attract young families because their community may no longer be attractive to young adults. Moreover, it may be difficult for a congregation to run the programs it once prided itself on because only seniors create most of the congregation, and there are—few, if any—young people to pass on this knowledge or bear the burden of the work.

The second change in the congregation's ecology that can produce congregational change is when the community's racial and/or ethic demographic changes. Originally, this ecological change was only seen as a problem for historic white churches in cities where minorities became the majority. These white churches faced the existential question of whether they would adapt to their black and brown residents or sell their property and relocate to a demographic they had more experience in reaching. Nevertheless, this is no longer the case because many African American congregations in the north and west are addressing their cities' transformation into a growing Latino demographic and reverse migration of African Americans to the South.[54] Consequently, African American congregations have to grapple with the question of whether they should change and adapt or move to reach their traditional demographic.[55]

These changes in a congregational ecology can cause a local church to be severely affected in adverse ways because these changes can produce anxiety over membership and revenue decline, and heated discussions over whether a congregation should alter its culture to meet the new challenge or act as if nothing is occurring as if nothing is occurring. Oftentimes destructive church conflicts can be led by long-time members who may not want any change in church culture—even when it is needed—because it was that church culture that attracted them to join the church years ago under a beloved former pastor. Consequently, most heated church disputes are internal disagreements on how the church should face the challenges of congregational change.

Pastoral Transitions

Pastoral transitions are an internal change within a congregation that is a major congregational stressor, which can trigger destructive conflict in a local church for two reasons. First, pastoral transitions affect the entire congregational system—in a general sense—simply because a "change in one part [of the congregation] produces change in another part, even in the whole."[56] However, the question remains: Why do pastoral transitions not only affect parts of the local church, but sometimes an entire church in a negative way? Peter Steinke gives insight into the answer when he wrote in *Health Congregations* that "Both organism and organizations are more apt to become sick after major losses, disruptive events, and prominent changes. All put stress on a system's balance."[57]

Certainly, a transition in the senior pastoral leadership of a local church is a "prominent" change for a congregation that can even be a "disruptive event" and/or an experience of major loss.[58] Conversely, if a congregation has had a very loving relationship with a former senior pastor—especially if the pastoral tenure was long and prosperous—the departure of the former pastor through death or resignation will cause a local church to go through a season of congregational grieving that may cause the church to manifest unhealthy behaviors that can make it sick.[59] Similar to how individuals can manifest the stages of grief such as anger, denial, or extreme sadness before they accept that a natural transition of life has permanently occurred, churches as organizational systems can do the same before they accept that a pastoral transition has truly happened.[60] Congregations that have had a loving and productive relationship with their previous pastor can lose sight of "who they are" as the people of God, "what they are about as a community" codified in their church mission, and the "extreme attention" upon the former pastor becomes a "matter of idealizing clergy."[61] One of the sickness that this particular church experiences is that the members behave as if the church cannot progress without the previous pastor's presence and practices at the helm. This over-idealization of the previous pastoral leadership is itself a manifestation of congregational grief.[62]

Consequently, a new pastor should not expect to move immediately into the hearts of the membership as their spiritual and corporate leader in the full sense upon appointment, any more than a stepparent can be expected to be seen as a full-fledged parent over a stepchild when a blended family is initially created. New pastors who push for immediate acceptance or congregational change too early in their pastoral tenure will—most likely—be met with entrenched resistance and possible rejection by their church membership, triggering destructive conflict. This is because some will interpret a swift embrace of the new pastor and his vision as disloyalty to the previous pastoral leadership.

In contrast, if the new pastor has replaced a former pastor who the congregation strongly disliked, there will probably be a residual of bitterness, anger, and mistrust of the pastoral office in general that the new pastor may have to endure for a season. Indeed, just as people can display trust issues and scarring from a bitter divorce from a former spouse, congregations can manifest the same behavior because—oftentimes—a forced pastoral resignation due to a bad pastor-congregation fit can be a form of an ecclesiastical divorce. The lack of cooperation between the church members and the former pastor can be interpreted—rightly or wrongly—as a rejection of that pastor as their spiritual leader, and the former pastor's resignation can be interpreted—rightly or wrongly—as a rejection of the church members of a congregation. In this church experience, the over-focus upon the disliked former pastor causes members to over-fixate on one part of the system (the former pastor), which, makes it "difficult [for the membership] to see the rest of the system." [63] This reality will cause the congregation to fail to focus and understand its mission and embrace the new opportunity they have with their new spiritual leader.

Second, pastoral transitions are congregational stressors—in a particular sense—because they frequently create church culture clashes between the pastor and the membership that spark destructive church conflict. Clergy should be aware of the "pastoral affect" upon local churches. This means that every pastor is a "culture carrier" because their pastoral ministries internalize the practices, beliefs, and ethos of the former pastor and/or congregation that made the biggest spiritual effect in their lives and faith whether they were conscious of it or not.[64] Therefore, whenever there is a new pastor—by retirement, death, or resignation—the local church's organizational culture will inevitably change to some degree. If the new pastor is a spiritual product of a congregation as a ministerial "son", the local church's cultural transformation in the new pastoral administration will probably be less acute. This is the case, because the new pastor who is a spiritual product of the congregation, he now leads has most likely "naturally and almost unconsciously absorbed that culture over time."[65] Nevertheless, if the opposite is the case, the organizational culture shift will be far-reaching, making some long-time members feel as if they no longer recognize and/or feel at home in "their" church. This is because the culture that the new pastor brings conflicts with the existing culture of the congregation that proceeded the pastor's tenure. As a result, the potential for serious congregational conflict to emerge in a local church is significantly high in the first couple years of a pastoral transition and even more so if this transition happened in not-so-great terms that involved a scandal of some kind.

In contrast, destructive congregational conflict in pastoral transitions can be avoided if the new pastor focuses more on building trust in the early years of their tenure rather than merely pushing their new pastoral vision. The trust-building practice of the new pastor should include understanding the existing church culture before the new pastor initiates change, even if that change is desperately needed. By doing this, the new pastor will gain "relational power" that is "even stronger than formal power" that is codified in the denomination's constitution or in their title as pastor.[66] Burns, Chapman, and Gunthrie noted why "relational power" is so critical for a pastor when they wrote, "Through the development of trust and respect in relationships, people earn the right to be heard and thus gain relational power to lead…relationships usually delineate what people are and are not able to. 'Leadership is not a title.' The right to lead is earned. And it takes a while."[67]

Consequently, if a new pastor wants to be a transformational leader who brings about enduring change instead of devastating conflict, the pastor must enter their office by pacing themselves and focusing on paying their dues to become pastor both in word and deed. Time is really on the pastor's side if they exercise patience and embrace the idea of success over the long term.

Furthermore, congregational leaders need to be mature to understand that it is not a matter of if their church will change, but what kind of change do they want to have: peaceful or volatile. If congregational leaders are flexible and embrace the new culture the pastor brings in—assuming it is biblical—it will make it easier for the remainder of the local church to do the same. Congregational leaders—appointed, elected, and unofficial—will have more influence than the new pastor does because they will have more "relational power" with the members of the local church.[68] Good church leaders are aware of this and do not seek to abuse their influence but use it to give the new pastor an opportunity to gain ground for the good of the church. This proper use of church leader's influence also includes helping anxious members "manage their disturbing feelings" who confide in them.[69] Therefore, seasoned church leaders can facilitate embracing this change because they are "the stewards of the congregational unit" and it is their biblical responsibility to do this.[70]

Professional Breaches of Congregational Trust

Another major congregational stressor is a breach in congregational trust by a clergy or lay leader within a local church that can cause severe, destructive church conflict. A clergy member who has been licensed and/or ordained has received the confidence of their congregation—their pastor if they are an elder without charge—and their jurisdictional bishop not only to declare the faith but also embody it in their daily conduct. This expectation of consecrated conduct is articulated within the COGIC ordination vows when the bishop explicitly asks an ordination candidate, "Will you be diligent in prayer and fasting, in the reading and doing what is contained in the Holy Scriptures."[86]

In a similar way, lay leaders of local churches who their pastor appoints and/or who their congregation elects to serve in positions in their churches accepted a sacred trust from their pastor and fellow congregants to be morally and ethically congruent with the Christian faith as well. When a person receives a position in a local church—whether they know it or not—they become representatives of that congregation in the community in which they reside. People in the lay leader's community who will never step into the doors of the congregation of which they are a member will—rightly or wrongly—judge the authenticity of their church's witness through the conduct these lay leaders display before them. Therefore, the sacred trust their congregation and denomination place within clergy and lay leaders is not an unrealistic expectation for them to be paradigms of perfection because all human beings are deeply flawed by the depravity of sin. To the contrary, it is expected that clergy and lay leaders be paradigms of true piety, which entails basic moral and ethical behavior, and an earnest commitment to contribute to a church climate that fosters healing, wholeness, and holiness. Simply put, they are expected to "walk worthy of the vocation wherewith [they] are called" (Ephesians 4:1). By doing so, clergy and lay leaders are "leading from the front" as examples of what it means to "follow peace with all men" and live a life of "holiness without which no one will see the Lord" (Hebrews 12:14).

Regrettably, sometimes clergy and lay leaders do not "walk worthy of the vocation wherewith [they] are called" and violate the confidence that was entrusted to them in shameful conduct. This shameful behavior of clergy and lay leaders usually manifests itself in two areas: sexual misconduct and the misappropriation of church's money and property for personal gain. These disgraceful acts by church leaders—especially clergy—are professional breaches in congregational trust because these behaviors betray the denomination and the congregation's confidence whenever they are committed.

Professional breaches of congregational trust are notorious congregational stressors that cause church conflict in several ways. First, professional breaches of congregational trust elicit destructive congregational conflict because it divides a church into factions.[72] This is the case for two reasons. First, church members and ecclesiastical leaders who are entangled in the vortex of dealing with breaches of conflict within a congregation are torn on whether to side with or oppose the person accused of such actions. Oftentimes, the acknowledgment that all Christians have sinned can cause one faction of the congregation to side with the clergy or lay leader from the position that no one is perfect, and the church should be merciful to the accused perpetrator. The problem with this argument is that sinless perfection is not needed for a lay leader or clergy to act with integrity and not misuse funds or engage in inappropriate sexual relations with persons within the congregation. In addition, when the church only calls for mercy for the fallen lay leader or clergy, is it being unintentionally unmerciful to the victim—who has less power—or the congregation that has suffered the most from the corrupt conduct. The other faction that may divide the church in destructive conflict is that some members will feel that the actions of a fallen clergy and lay leader have betrayed them, and they want the ecclesiastical and civil law to hold accountable the person who acted in professional misconduct.

Second, professional breaches of congregational trust are congregational stressors that create conflict because church leaders' scandalous actions cause some in leadership and the congregation to go display an avoidance conflict resolution posture to the congregation's detriment. Scandals create the overwhelming temptation for the congregation and the bishop to "bury one's head in the sand" in the name of "waiting on God" and/or hoping that the bad news about the clergy or lay leader will go away or improve over time. When this occurs, these church members who feel the fallen church leader has betrayed them will also feel the ecclesiastical leadership betrayed them because they seek to evade holding the perpetrator accountable through ignoring the obvious before their own eyes. Unfortunately, professional breaches of congregational trust have severely marred COGIC's ecclesiastical reputation, breaches which have inundated the Internet with the documented many fallen clergy and lay leader's disgraceful deeds. The result of these cases has cost the denomination millions and has thrust many churches into turmoil and damage that last for decades.

Transgression in Boundaries Concerning Power

The final congregational stressor that can lead to destructive congregational conflict is a perceived transgression in boundaries concerning power. Bylaws, job descriptions, and procedure manuals help define boundaries or power within any organization. Whenever boundaries are not understood, defined conflicts will certainly arise. The COGIC has a constitution that governs our church, but many clergy are barely knowledgeable of its content. Moreover, most laypersons have not even read the COGIC Constitution. In addition, since most of our churches are less than 100 members, many of them operate informally without defined roles and operations that make them vulnerable to congregational discord. Although the COGIC Constitution allows for local churches to have bylaws that are not repugnant to that of the international church, many COGIC congregations do not have one in place.[73] Moreover, those COGIC congregations that do have local church bylaws, often have bylaws that have not been seen by most members within the local church that governs them. Therefore, when people do not know their roles, someone is bound to transgress into another's role.

Some COGIC pastors mistakenly believe that just because they are made the president/ "chief executive officer" (CEO) of a COGIC congregation by ecclesiastical appointment, the office of CEO gives them unlimited power within the church they lead; it does not.[74] COGIC pastors cannot unilaterally remove trustee members contrary to the laws of their state or use church funds without the consent of their Board of Trustees.[75] COGIC pastors have the authority to appoint and remove spiritual officers (e.g., ministers of music, lay leaders, ministers, deacons, and elders), but the officers who govern the temporal assets of the church (e.g., trustees) are beyond the pastors' reach. Most of the destructive church conflicts that have erupted in COGIC congregations regarding church finances and property have occurred because these healthy boundaries were not understood and maintained.

Conclusion

This chapter has argued that church leaders and laity must have a mature perspective of church conflicts that views disputes within churches as a natural part of congregational life, which on its own does not have to be destructive and negative. In fact, it has been shown that when church conflict is handled properly, it can be the event that causes a church to think deeply about its current realities, contemplate its mission, and seek change, which can produce congregational renewal. Nevertheless, this chapter has also regrettably shown that there is a hard truth about church conflict rooted in our humanity. This truth is that the sinfulness of human nature even among Christians does cause destructive conflict to emerge in churches that congregational stressors trigger. The congregational stressors are usually internal or external factors that cause congregational change, professional breaches in congregational trust, and transgression or boundaries related to power. When these events occur, the earthly Zion of the church finds it difficult to sing as it used to sing, or shout as it used to shout because it becomes trapped in the vortex of conflict.

CHAPTER II

[1] "O Zion (What's the Matter Now)," African American Pentecostal Call and Response Praise Song.

[2] Kenneth Haugk, *Antagonist in the Church: How to Identify and Deal with Destructive Conflict* (Minneapolis: Augsburg Publishing House, 1988), 31.

[3] Charles Wesley, "A Charge I Have to Keep," in Yes Lord! Church of God in Christ Hymnal, ed. (Memphis: The Church of God in Christ Publishing Board, 1982), 330.

[4] Thabiti Anyabwile and Isaac Adams, "The Difference between a Healthy and Peaceful Church," *The Front Porch,* January 9, 2016, https://thefrontporch.org/2016/02/the-difference-between-a-healthy-and-a-peaceful-church/.

[5] Ibid.

[6] Ibid.

[7] Michael Hare, *When Church Conflict Happens: A Proven Process for Resolving Unhealthy Disagreements and Embracing Healthy Ones* (Chicago: Moody Publishers, 2019), 34.

[8] Lee G. Bolman and Terrence E. Deal, *Reframing Organizations: Artistry, Choice, and Leadership* (San Francisco: John Wiley and Sons, Inc., 2003), 198.

[9] Norma Cook Everist, *Church Conflict: From Contention to Collaboration* (Nashville: Abingdon Press, 2004), 20.

[10] Ibid., 20.

[11] Ibid., 17.

[12] I show my indebtedness to conceptualizing the Church as the image of the Trinity from the writings of Greek Orthodox bishop and theologian John D. Zizioulas. He writes that the Church is more than an institution but a "mode of existence," a way of being"; cf. John D. Zizioulas, *Being as*

Communion: Studies in Personhood and the Church (Crestwood: St. Vladimir's Seminary Press, 1985), 15. He further writes that, "In the eucharist the Church becomes a reflection if the eschatological community of Christ, the Messiah, an image of the Trinitarian life of God. In terms of human existence this mainly means one thing: the transcendence of all divisions, both natural and social, which keep the existence of the world in a state of disintegration, fragmentation, decomposition and hence death" (cf. Ibid., 254-55). Therefore, it is only when the Church takes on a "way of being" that it mirrors in a creaturely appropriate way the oneness of the Trinitarian persons so that it—by grace—can transcend "all divisions, both natural and social (cf. Ibid., 15, 254-55).

[13] Jason Firch, "Church and Religious Charitable Giving Statistics," Nonprofit Source, 2020, https://nonprofitssource.com/online-giving-statistics/church-giving/.

[14] The Pew Research Group notes that only 43% of adults volunteer in churches and 57% do so in the Church of God in Christ, Inc., which is slightly higher than other evangelical denominations; Alexander Sandstrom, "Church Involvement Varies Widely among US Christians," Pew Research Group, last modified November 16, 2015, https://www.pewresearch.org/fact-tank/2015/11/16/church-involvement-varies-widely-among-u-s-christians/.

[15] Aaron Earls, "The Church Growth Gap: The Big Get Bigger and the Small Get Smaller," *Christianity Today*, March 6, 2019, https://www.christianitytoday.com/news/2019/march/lifeway-research-church-growth-attendance-size.html.

[16] The political frame of organizational analysis maintains that "the combination of scarce resources and divergent interests produces conflict as surely as night follows day" (cf. Bolman and Deal, *Reframing Organizations,* 197).

[17] Ibid., 190.

[18] Bob Burns, Tasha D. Chapman, and Donald C. Guthrie, *The Politics of Ministry: Navigating Power Dynamics and Negotiating Interest* (Downers Grove: InterVarsity Press, 2019), 12-13.

[19] Bolman and Deal, *Reframing Organizations,* 190.

[20] Martin Luther coined this Latin phrase to signify the biblical truth that Christians are righteous because of their justification by faith and sinners whose depravity remains even after conversion.

[21] John T. McNeill, ed., *Calvin Christian Institutes of Religion Book II* (Philadelphia: The Westminster Press, 1960), 252.

[22] Timothy F. Lull, ed., "Bondage of the Will," in *Martin Luther's Basic Theological Writings* (Minneapolis: Fortress Press, 1989), 185.

[23] Alfred Poirier, *The Peace-Making Pastor: A Biblical Guide to Resolving Church Conflict* (Grand Rapids: Baker Books, 2006), 53.

[24] A. Z. Hall, ed., *Church of God in Christ Minutes of the General Assembly 1934-1960* (Memphis: Church of God in Christ Publishing House, 2001), X.

[25] Ibid., X.

[26] Elton H. Weaver III, *Bishop Charles H. Mason in the Age of Jim Crow: The Struggle for Religious and Moral Uplift* (Lanham: Lexington Books, 2020), 239.

[27] Ibid.

[28] Ibid.

[29] Ibid.

[30] Ibid.

[31] Ibid.

[32] Ibid.

[33] Kenneth O. Gangel and Samuel L. Canine, *Communication and Conflict Management in Churches and Christian Organizations* (Nashville: Broadman Press, 1992), 53.

[34] John Burnaby, ed., "The Spirit and the Letter," in *Augustine: Later Works* (Philadelphia: The Westminster Press, 1955), 196.

[35] Ibid., 195.

[36] It is here that I show my indebtedness to Steinke's biological model applied to local congregations; cf. Peter L. Steinke, *Healthy Congregations: A Systems Approach* (Lanham: Rowman and Litchfield, 1996), 28.

[37] Ibid., 23.

[38] Geffrey B. Kelley, ed., Life *Together* (Minneapolis: Fortress Press, 1996), 35.

[39] Steinke, *Healthy Congregations,* 4, 8.

[40] Ibid., 19.

[41] Steinke calls this part of the brain the R-system or reptilian brain, which is the lowest part of the brain (cf. Ibid., 69-70).

[42] Ibid., 68.

[43] Ibid., 4, 19.

[44] Ibid., 69.

[45] Ibid., 19.

[46] Ibid., 61. Triangulation is defined by Bixby as the moment when "at least three people interact with each other about a particular issue"; Doug Bixby, *Navigating the Nonsense: Church Conflict and Triangulation* (Eugene: Cascade Books, 2016), xvii.

[47] Steinke, *Health Congregations,* 62.

[48] Haugk, *Antagonist in the Church,* 32.

[49] Bixby, *Navigating the Nonsense,* xvii-xviii.

[50] Haugk, *Antagonist in the Church,* 32.

[51] Congregational ecology refers to a "particular neighborhood [or] region" in which a church is located and from "which [the local church] likely draws members and participants." It also refers to "economic and political institutions that create the jobs and build the roads that bring people to the doorstep [of your congregation] (or take them away) from it"; cf. Nancy T. Ammerman et al., *Studying Congregation: A New Handbook* (Nashville: Abingdon Press, 1998), 14.

[52] The Great Migration of the twentieth century among African Americans is a great example of this phenomenon. Because African Americans could not thrive in the segregated South, millions of them relocated to the American North and West. This exodus transformed the COGIC from a southern church with members mostly in the Mid-South, to a national denomination with strong churches in America's metropolitan areas.

[53] Steinke, *Healthy Congregation,* 4.

[54] Sisson, Carmen K. "Why African-Americans Are Moving Back to the South." *The Christian Science Monitor,* March 16, 2014. https://www.csmonitor.com/USA/Society/2014/0316/Why-African-Americans-are-moving-back-to-the-South.

[55] An example of this can be found concerning the St. Stephen's Cathedral Church of God in Christ in San Diego, California, during the pastoral ministry of the late Bishop George Dallas McKinney, PhD; Adrian Florido, "Feeling a Different Pulse in the Heart of Black San Diego," *Voice of San Diego,* March 13, 2011, https://www.voiceofsandiego.org/neighborhoods/feeling-a-different-pulse-in-the-heart-of-black-san-diego/.

[56] Steinke, *Healthy Congregations,* 4.

[57] Ibid., 17.

[58] This is especially true if the pastoral transition was brought about by death or the unexpected resignation of a gifted pastoral leader (cf. Ibid., 17); Haugk, *Antagonist in the Church,* 4, 8.

[59] As Peter Steinke notes, churches are emotional systems; cf. Steinke, *Healthy Congregations,* 8-9. Just as individuals can manifest the stages of grief like anger, denial, or extreme sadness before they accept that a natural transition of life has permanently occurred, churches can do the same; Laundale Monroe, "Family Systems in Congregational Settings," *Ministry: International Journal for Pastors,* June 2009, https://www.ministrymagazine.org/archive/2009/06/family-systems.

[60] Vanderbloen, "How to Deal with the Unexpected Loss of a Pastor," July 1, 2017, https://www.vanderbloemen.com/blog/unexpected-loss-pastor; and Michelle Lauzurek, "When the Pastor You Love Leaves Your Church," *Crosswalk*, November 19, 2018, https://www.crosswalk.com/church/pastors-or-leadership/when-the-pastor-you-love-leaves-your-church-10-ways-to-navigate-pastoral-transition.html.

[61] Steinke, *Healthy Congregations,* 45.

[62] People tend to over-idealize the deceased loved one and not remember their failing and faults. This is also done with beloved former pastors who become the "heroes" in the history of a congregation's narrative about itself.

[63] Ibid., 45.

[64] Aubrey Malphurs, *Look Before You Lead: How to Discern and Shape Your Church Culture* (Grand Rapids: Baker Books, 2013), 98.

[65] Ibid., 98.

[66] Burns, Chapman, and Gunthrie, *The Politics of Ministry,* 43.

[67] Ibid., 46.

[68] Burns, Chapman, and Gunthrie, *The Politics of Ministry,* 43-44.

[69] Steinke, *Healthy Congregations,* 28.

[70] Ibid., 28.

[71] C. F. Range Jr., ed., *Church of God in Christ Official Manual* (Memphis: Church of God in Christ Publishing House, 1973), 209.

[72] Pamela Cooper-White notes that churches are usually torn asunder by sexual misconduct because, "The parish is left to cope with feelings of betrayal and rage, which are often directed at the woman as seductress" (Ibid., 131).

[73] Range Jr., *Church of God Official Manual,* 81.

[74] Ibid., 26.

[75] Ibid., 81.

CHAPTER THREE

"EVERYTHING GOING DOWN BUT THE WORD OF GOD"

Corporate boardrooms and secular governments frequently use conflict resolution teams as agents of mitigation and reconciliation, but does the Church have biblical support to use this tool for use in COGIC congregations? This project cannot evade this important question because COGIC congregations and bishops will swiftly dismiss a CCRT as another secular tool mistakenly imported into the Church if they cannot effectively articulate the biblical and theological justification for its existence and work. Nevertheless, the question remains: Why is a biblical mandate for a CCRT so imperative for its implementation within the denomination? Furthermore, what are the conditions by which we can determine a CCRT as biblical without defining what it means to be biblical? Unfortunately, we live in a day when the term "biblical" is casually used in a flippant manner that has lost meaning even within the Church. These two critical questions will be answered before we explore the biblical passages that will show that a CCRT is indeed congruent with Scripture and deserving of being called a biblical model for conflict resolution.

First, biblical support is essential to implementing a CCRT

because the denomination has historically prided itself on not only being Spirit-led, but biblically driven in its beliefs and modus operandi. This fact reflects COGIC's high view of Scripture, which demands that the "Word of God to be the only authority in all matters"—and certainly one of these critical "matters" would include how the Church resolves its disputes when it is confronted with conflict.[1] Moreover, if a practice's biblical foundation cannot be affirmed through a "careful investigation of the meaning of particular [biblical] passages" rightly divided, then COGIC theology seriously questions whether it is a Spirit-driven practice for God's people. The ability to make such an assessment is essential to a denomination birthed within the flames of fervent pneumatological renewal in the late nineteenth and early twentieth centuries.[2] For consideration, how can the harmonious coherence of Scripture and Spirit-driven practice be denied when God the Holy Spirit—the third person of the Trinity—is the divine author of the Scriptures? Consequently, this affirmation makes COGIC—people of both the book (the Bible) and the Holy Spirit—because they read and theologize the Scriptures in, with, and through the Spirit.[3]

Further, note that the very *lex orandi* of the COGIC found in its prayers, hymns, and praise songs are congruent with its official theology on this matter. When the saints raise their voices in transcendent power and sing, "Everything is going down but the Word of God"—the same kind of power that the late James Baldwin recollects that would make churches of his memory "rock"—this very song that they sing embodies COGIC's rich theology concerning the Bible.[4] Indeed, truth is conveyed despite the brevity of the song's lyrics that, everything (e.g., people, nations, institutions, and even models for ecclesiastical use) are transitory and cannot be trusted unless they are firmly rooted in the Word of God that endures forever.[5]

In contrast, the very definition of the word "biblical" is also necessary to answer the question about whether a CCRT can be considered biblical. This is an important act because oftentimes, those who use the term "biblical"—especially within the wider Evangelical Protestant tradition —assume that others who use it have the same theological meaning, which may not be the case. This is most apparent when we see two individuals in passionate disagreement claiming to be advocating a "biblical" teaching despite having two conflicting theological claims. In this scenario, the error is not found within the Bible that they used, but in someone's reading of it. In all cases, equal attention must be focused upon the reader and the reading of the Bible as well as the passages they cite and the theological claims they make.

Certainly, to be "biblical" is more than simply collecting and citing biblical passages in theological and exegetical isolation by an individual who believes that such passages support their view. Whenever a person uses the Bible in this way, they do not consider the historical and exegetical context of the verses they cite and being in prayerful conversation with how the Church—both universally and confessionally—has understood these passages; that person—no matter how sincere—reads the Scriptures in isolation, which leads to hermeneutical error. Such readings of Scripture usually tell us more about the individual reader than it does about the Bible whose verses they passionately quote. Ironically, the people who do isolationist biblical interpretation the best are the heterodox and heretical religious movements that distort the Bible isogetically to invent all sorts of damnable religious innovations that put the soul in peril. These misguided persons quoting a multitude of Bible verses in isolation may truly be called biblicist—in that they grasp the Bible to prostitute the biblical text—but their teachings cannot be considered authentically biblical in nature.

Consequently, this project will consider the idea of a CCRT as biblical considering how it has been previously defined in this chapter. This means that a biblical designation of this model will consider simultaneously and put into conversation Scripture, the theological tradition, reason, and experience.[6] First, the conflict resolution model will be considered "biblical" in that it can be congruent with the Scriptural teachings concerning conflict and reconciliation. This congruency with Scripture will be inferred through a careful examination of three biblical passages where these teachings are the most explicit. Here, this project is being transparent that certain judgements will be made as to which biblical passages best summarize the overall Scriptural teaching on the matter. This hermeneutical judgment is done for two significant reasons. First, a harmony must be imposed upon numerous biblical passages that exist in several Biblical texts with their unique and differing historical context. In this sense, I will look at these passages primarily as a theologian more than a scholar in biblical studies. However, this should not be interpreted that the knowledge from the historical critical method will not be used when deemed helpful to illuminate insights into our study. Conversely, such hermeneutical judgments will be made to constrain the limits of our inquiry so that it does not drift beyond our research are. Second, we read the biblical passages considering the Church's—both in its universal and denominational expressions—concerning reconciliation and conflict contained in the theological tradition. I am a member of the universal Church, the Protestant Reformation, and a Holiness-Pentecostal as a member of the COGIC; therefore, it should not be surprising if these elements inform the final designation of the model's biblical quality that we present in dialogue with the Christian tradition in all these dimensions. Finally, this project will use an intellectual process rooted in reason, that by grace, the Holy Spirit will illuminate.

"A Threefold Cord": An Old Testament Support for Team Effort

Ironically, biblical support for using a team approach for conflict resolution can be inferred from a passage in the not-so-widely read Book of Ecclesiastes or Koheleth, as it is known in the

Hebrew Bible.[7] Ecclesiastes only identifies the author as a "son of David, king of Jerusalem," but the actual name of the writer of this book within the canon of Scripture is unknown (Ecclesiastes 1:1). Therefore, we are left to concur with most Biblical scholars that the "teacher" or sage who penned Ecclesiastes was an anonymous writer who was nonetheless inspired by the Holy Spirit to convey to his readers heavenly wisdom gained from earthly experience (II Timothy 3:16).[98]

The sage or teacher of Ecclesiastes gives biblical support to the assertion that lives are best lived, and tasks are best accomplished when they are lived and done with others, as opposed to those that are lived and done alone. This is the sage's conviction because his life observations has convinced him that a person who is "alone, without companion" or "son nor brother" is "vanity and a grave misfortune" (Ecclesiastes 4:8 NKJV).[9] Why does the sage give such a positive view of team living as opposed to those who operate and/or live in isolation? The answer to this question can be discerned from the examples that he cites in the text of Chapter 4. He says that it is possible to defeat one person alone, but it is more difficult to defeat two persons together because the "two can withstand" their common enemy (Ecclesiastes 4:10, 12 NKJV). The writer also notes that experience has shown him that those who have a friend can be lifted by them in adversity (Ecclesiastes 4:10). In addition, the sage in Ecclesiastes states—in contradistinction to the one who has a friend— "woe to [the one] who is alone when he falls, for he has no one to help him" (Ecclesiastes 4:10 NKJV). Consequently, the sage asserts emphatically that, "Two are better than one, because they have a good reward for their labor" (Ecclesiastes 4:9).

The Book of Ecclesiastes maintains that living and working alone is a gross misfortune because the sage recognizes strength in personal and working teams. Therefore, he concludes that, a "threefold cord is not easily broken," which is another way of saying that those things done with others are not so easily undone (Ecclesiastes 4:9, 12 NKJV).

Some may dismiss the biblical sage's observation on the importance of teams in tasks as having no special significance because it is one view among many. Unfortunately, all views gleaned from life experiences in our post-modern world are considered equally authoritative. However, Frick argues that, the Hebraic Faith that Christians inherited from the prophets, priest, and sages considered their recorded wisdom in the biblical canon to have originated from God "like the priestly Torah and the prophetic word."[10] This was the case because the Ancient Israelites who penned the Hebrew Bible—which Christians call the Old Testament—believed their faith came from God through the mediums of the priest, prophet, and the sage.[11] This is why the ancient Judeans skeptical of Jeremiah's prophetic warnings mocked him by saying that, "the teaching of the law by the priest will not cease, nor will counsel from the wise [the sage], nor the word from the prophets" (Jeremiah 18:18 NIV). This was the case because there was no such thing as secular wisdom in Ancient Israel considering faith and knowledge were thoroughly intertwined.[12] Hebrew Bible scholar Gerhard von Rad put it this way, "Israel knew nothing of the aporia which we read into these proverbs. It was perhaps her greatness that she did not keep faith and knowledge apart. The experience of the world was for her always divine experiences as well, and the experiences of God were for her experiences of the world."[13]

Therefore, the writer of Ecclesiastes recorded not just wise sayings—equal to any sayings we deem wise—but divinely inspired wisdom that is profitable for us today (I Corinthians 6:11).

In summary, there are three factors that we can summarize about Ecclesiastes that are significant to this project. First, considering the biblical writer in the Book of Ecclesiastes argues that tasks are best accomplished when not attempted alone, the greatest task that a pastor and/or a congregation will face is to avoid and/or resolve destructive church conflict. The pastor and congregation should not face this enemy of conflict alone but with a trained and prayerful team that can help them withstand this ecclesiastical threat together. Second, the team approach is the prudent one for church conflict because oftentimes, the solutions that emerge from a group rather than from an individual is the metaphorical "threefold cord" that is not time and situations do not easily break. The more decisions emerge from a team of individuals within a congregation who have prayerfully reflected upon a situation of a local church in the crisis of conflict, the stronger it will be because everyone will bring their unique skill set and experiences into a symphony that is usually the most prudent.

Examples of Conflict Resolution in the Pauline Churches

The New Testament is inundated with numerous examples of heated disputes within the Pauline Churches that provide insights into how to construct a biblical model of conflict resolution. Certainly, we could easily exceed this project's scope if we attempted to examine all the examples of conflict within the Pauline communities contained within the New Testament. Nevertheless, a critical question can be raised: Why were the churches that Paul established so prone to conflict, other than that they were comprised of fallen human beings who had embraced Jesus as Lord and Christ?

Pauline congregations were frequently susceptible to conflict because the Apostle Paul pastored the churches recorded in the New Testament primarily *in absentia*.[14] This was the case because Paul established numerous congregations within "private houses" in the major Greco-Roman cities and moved on to plant others in new urban locations.[15] His estimated travel mileage during his apostolic career was "nearly ten thousand miles" on roads and sea in which he encountered "government officials, traders, pilgrims, the sick, letter-carriers, sightseers, runaway slaves, fugitives, prisoners, athletes, artisans, teachers, and students" with the gospel message.[16] In fact, the longest time the sainted apostle spent with any congregation was a period of three years. The churches that Paul established did not often have the benefit of his physical presence to confront rival missionaries with contrary doctrinal views or to mediate between interpersonal disputes among the faithful. It is accurate to say that Paul primarily pastored via his prolific pen that wrote letters that made known revelations, clarified doctrine, settled disputes, and enacted discipline when it was needed to restore order in fractured congregations. This use of the letter was a conventional practice in the Greco-Roman world.[17] Indeed, Paul's modus operandi of pastoral leadership in absentia would be challenging in the twenty-first century with all its technological aides, not alone in the First Century of the Common Era when these modern ministry tools did not exist.

An interesting example of conflict and conflict resolution within a Pauline congregation can be found in Paul's letter to the Philippians. Paul had been informed that the harmony of the church at Philippi had been broken by an interpersonal contention between two gifted female Christian leaders within the Philippian congregation: Euodia and Syntche (Philippians 4:2-3).[18] We can infer the giftedness and importance of these two women to the Philippian congregation by the fact that women were rarely mentioned directly by name in Greco-Roman documents by either secular and/or religious writers.[19] This alone should cause the reader of this Pauline text to take note of these two women's significance. Also, Paul removes any doubt as to Euodia and Syntche's prominence when he states directly that these two women were among those who "struggled beside me in the work of the gospel," most probably being among his "first converts" in Philippi (Philippians 4:3 NRSV).[20] Paul's words suggest that he esteemed these women as congregational leaders. The apostle's words conveyed the fact that Euodia and Syntyche worked in ministry equally with other co-laborers whom he valued, even though Paul was the Philippian congregation's senior leader and establishmentarian. New Testament scholar Elisabeth Schussler Fiorenza concurs with this when she writes, "It is significant, therefore, that Paul uses the same Greek verb, kopian, "to labor" or "toil," not only to characterize his own evangelizing and teaching but also that of women." Fiorenza further asserts that "Paul also affirms that women worked with him [Paul] on an equal basis. Phil 4:2–3 explicitly states that Euodia and Syntyche have 'contended' side by side with him."[21]

The knowledge of the contention between these women may have come to Paul through earlier correspondence to the Apostle Paul from a concerned individual within the church and/or the Philippian Christians as a whole (I Corinthians 1:11).[22] We cannot be certain as to the exact means by which Paul was informed because not all the letters between Paul and his churches are found in the New Testament canon.[23] It is certain, even though we do not have all the historical facts, that the congregation wrote to Paul to express their collective concern for his personal well-being while he was under house arrest and the possibility of his release was uncertain at best or doubtful at worst (Philippians 4:10).[24] Although the Philippian congregation was concerned as to whether Paul was "amply supplied" by the financial "gifts" that they had sent to him, Paul told them that his prior experience in ministry had taught him "the secret of being content in any and every situation, whether well fed or hungry, whether living in plenty or in want" (Philippians 4:12 NIV). Surprisingly, the primary concern of the apostle under house arrest for a capital offense was not temporal and/or personal, but rather pastoral. More than anything else, Paul's, concern for the Philippian Christians—now more than ever—was that they all be of the "same love, being one in spirit and of one mind" in the Lord (Philippians 2:2; 4:18 NIV).

We should take note not only of the content in Paul's conflict resolution in his letter to the Philippians (e.g., his words), but also of the strategic approach that Paul took to achieve that goal. First, Paul strategically engaged in conflict resolution between these two women by dealing with the dispute publicly before the entire Philippian congregation. This should not surprise us, as biblical scholar Wayne Meeks observed that acts of reconciliation were performed in the meetings.[25] The Apostle Paul dealt with the conflict between Euodia and Syntyche by addressing it in a public setting, most likely in a worship setting where his letters were read as the church's sermon on "the first day of the week" before the Lord's Supper.[26] It was common for Paul to instruct his churches to have his letters read "to all the brothers," meaning the entire congregation (I Thessalonians 5:17).[27] This was critical because it is certain that the conflict between Euodia and Syntche had spilled out beyond the two women to affect—and possibly infect—the entire Philippian congregation. Indeed, Paul reasoned that, as the conflict had become public, it needed to be corrected publicly so the boil of conflict could be exposed to the light of truth and moral authority.

Second, the Apostle Paul's conflict resolution approach was to use his sermonic letters in a twofold way. On the one hand, Paul's letter as sermon was used as an indirect and tactful way to correct Euodia and Syntche by making clear what proper behavior rooted in Christology is. This was accomplished when Paul reminded the congregation that the proper φρονῆτεa or "mind" or "understanding"[28] would be that which was the same as Christ that they worshipped as one in "the form of God" (Philippians 2:5-6). Paul argued that Jesus' ability to "humble himself" and "to become obedient" caused him to be "highly exalted" and "given a name above all names" (Philippians 2:5, 8). When the Philippian Christians take the example of Christ as a model and assume this αὐτὸ φρονῆτεa or "same mind," they will be able to "do all things without murmuring and arguing" (Philippians 2:14).[29] In summary, Paul was alluding with rhetorical prowess to the fact that the root of a conflict in the church may be interpersonal on the surface, but its genuine origin was a spiritual deficiency within the two women that had boiled over into the entire congregation. Consequently, Paul reasoned that, if Christology became the model for the Philippian's ecclesiology, not only would conflict end between Euodia and Syntche—although Paul had not mentioned their names at this point—it would also bring peace to Christians everywhere.

On the other hand, Paul's letter as sermon was used as a tool of conflict resolution by naming the source of the conflict within the Philippian congregation directly without ambiguity. Paul did this by writing: "I urge Euodia, and I urge Syntyche to be of the same mind in the Lord" (Philippians 4:2). It should be noted that Paul skillfully used the first part of the letter to focus on Christ as a model because it could be expected that the entire Philippian congregation claimed to love Him. When Paul says that he "urges" Euodia and Syntyche "to be of the same mind," he is attempting to make an emotional plea to use the two women's mutual love for him to motivate them to reconcile. If the two women have any φρονεῖν or "concern" for Paul in his confinement, then they will hear his plea and be of "one mind" and cease their dispute (Philippians 2:5, 4:10).[30]

Paul's conflict resolution approach in the case of Euodia and Syntyche is significant for our project in two ways. First, Paul's approach to conflict in his letter to the Philippians makes clear that the private, interpersonal conflict between Euodia and Syntche was indeed a public matter. Certainly, Paul could have sent private letters directly to address the interpersonal dispute of these two women without addressing them in a letter read publicly before the whole Philippian Church. Nevertheless, the sainted apostle decided not to deal with this dispute in such a discreet manner, and such a method of conflict resolution should not be seen as coincidental.

Paul's rationale for such public conflict resolution approach is twofold. On the one hand, Paul was astute enough to recognize that the whole congregation needed to be involved because the private quarrel of Euodia and Syntche, whatever it may have been, put the very existence of the Philippian Church in peril. This is probable because congregational conflict tempts members to choose sides, leading to fragmentation, and compels others to withdraw from public worship when they have a conflict avoidance personality, affecting congregational morale. Fiorenza agrees with this reasoning when she says, "Paul considers the authority of both women in the community at Philippi so great that he fears that their dissension could do serious damage to the Christian mission."[31] New Testament scholar Richard Meilick Jr. also agrees that the Philippian congregation obviously "faced a major crisis because of these women" and the conflict that they had.[32]

On the other hand, Paul had the wide-eyed awareness that conflicting Christians left alone to reconcile without assistance seldom do so because their human depravity resists reconciliation to maintain its own selfish ends. This is the case because the fallenness of Christians in opposition to each other frequently blinds them to their pride, deafens their ear to thoughtful listening, and makes their issue of contention an "idol" that must be obeyed at all costs, no matter the consequence to the opposing party or the local church as a whole.[33] Therefore, Paul's public manner in addressing the conflict of Euodia and Syntche was his shrewd but pastoral way to get the entire Philippian Church to own the responsibility of mediation and reconciliation between the two women as a corporate imperative that all within the church should accept.

Third, Paul's choice that his letter be read[34] during the Philippian Church's worship service during prayer suggests that he saw the conflict between Euodia and Syntche as one that was not merely interpersonal, but spiritual. This is congruent with Paul's theology, because his writings to other churches describe "dissensions and factions" as works of the flesh that are incongruent with the Holy Spirit (Galatians 5:26 NIV). In fact, Paul believed that "quarrels" among Christians that divide them give the appearance that Christ himself is divided because Christians are "the body of Christ" (I Corinthians 1:10-13). Therefore, it is exactly because Paul saw congregational conflict as a manifestation of low spirituality that he addressed it during worship so that the faithful could confront their failings and seek spiritual renewal through worship, prayer, and the Word of God, as articulated in his letter.

Conflict Resolution in the Matthean Gospel

The Gospel of Matthew 18:15-30 is a very important passage of Scripture in any discussion of conflict resolution in the Church because it is a biblical text that talks about a Christian being directly wronged by another. It is true that some have questioned whether it is misguided to apply Matthew 18:15-30 to congregational disputes because the nature of the sin of one disciple against another is not specified by the Gospel writer in this passage[35]. Nevertheless, this passage is completely appropriate to apply to church conflict resolution for two irrefutable reasons. On the one hand, most church disputes are rooted in sin. On the other, even if a church conflict happens not to emerge from human sinfulness—which is extremely rare—the consequences of a conflict erroneously handled by imperfect Christians can be sin.[36]

Consequently, Matthew 18:15-30 is relevant to our project for the construction of a biblical approach to congregational conflict for three significant reasons. First, Matthew is the only gospel writer that uses the word ἐκκλησία or "church" in his writings, and he does it only twice.[37] On the one hand, Matthew uses the word "church" when Jesus proclaims the indestructability of the church by the powers of darkness, termed the "Gates of Hades," when he speaks to Peter at Caesarea Philippi (Matthew 16:18). On the other, Matthew uses ἐκκλησία or "church" in his gospel when Jesus tells his disciples that, if private attempts to reconcile conflict between a brother or sister fail, then they are to "tell it to the church" (Matthew 18:17 NRSV). The latter use of ἐκκλησία or "church" in a Matthean saying of Jesus that focuses on disputes between disciples is a recognition that the community of disciples is not a sinless community, but *"a corpus mixtum"* that consists of false prophets, wolves in sheep's clothing (7:15), wheat and tares (13:36-43), clean and unclean fish (13:47-48), good and bad (cf. 22:10).[38] Therefore, since the visible church is "a corpus mixtum" of imperfect disciples—and some who are outright committed to corruption and sin—negative conflict is indeed a possibility within the church.

Moreover, the latter use of ἐκκλησία, or "church", in Matthew's Gospel not only infers that sin among disciples leads to disputes within the church, but it also suggests that conflict among Christians is more than a private matter; it is an act that demands ecclesiastical intervention and concern. This is the case because the way disputes are handled within the church is "part of our witness to the world that Jesus Christ makes possible a people who are able to live with one another in hope and peace" and that "Christ has given us the means of living with one another without the fear and violence that constitute human relations in the world," as William Willimon reminds us.[39] The linking of the word "church" with a passage that deals with overcoming disputes among Christians by the Gospel writer inspired by the Holy Spirit cannot be seen as coincidental. On the contrary, this fact must be seen as purposeful to show that reconciliation is intrinsic, not tangential, to ecclesiological identity. Therefore, Jesus said, "By this everyone will know that you are my disciples, if you love one another" (John 13:35). The visible Church is the gathered community of disciples, and discipleship is tied not only to the love of God, but to the love of other believers in Christ, which implies resolution of anything that threatens that love.

Second, Matthew 18:15-30 is significant because it records Jesus' direct instruction on how to ethically handle intra-church conflict within the Messianic community. Jesus' teaching about conflict between disciples is set within his many discourses in Matthew's Gospel that present him as the preeminent "righteous interpreter of the Law in all His teachings, especially ethics, as well as in his deeds."[40] Jesus' instruction on how to handle a disciple who has sinned against another is an example of how his ethical teaching guided the Matthean community of antiquity in similar ways as other individual Jewish rabbis' teachings directed the communities under their charge.[41] This is an example of Matthew's consistent re-Judaization of Jesus in his Gospel to target his mostly Jewish audience, who would have recognized the significance of the Semitic nuance of presenting Jesus as a teacher.[42]

What was the teaching of Jesus in Matthew's Gospel? Jesus says in Matthew 18 that conflicts between Christians occur because one of them has "sinned against" a fellow disciple (Matthew 18:15).[43] This verse informs us that it is possible not only to sin directly against God, but also to sin against a brother or sister and, in so doing, indirectly sin against God. Consequently, negative relational distance with fellow believers creates spiritual distance between us and God. Therefore, Matthew records Jesus as saying, "Therefore, if you are offering your gift at the altar and there remember that your brother or sister has something against you, leave your gift there in front of the altar. First go and be reconciled to them; then come and offer your gift" (Matthew 5:23-24 NIV).

The two disputing disciples should confidentially resolve their differences among themselves according to the commandment of Jesus (Matthew 18:15-16). However, this ideal is sometimes difficult to achieve because confronting a sister or brother concerning a fault in an attempt to reconcile differences with them may fail. Nevertheless, a disciple against whom another believer has sinned is not absolved of the sacred responsibility of godly confrontation by the commandment of Jesus in the text. The mostly Jewish original audience of Matthew knew—as Culpepper notes—that reproving a brother or sister in error is an "act of love" rooted in the core teaching of the *Torah*[44]. He writes,

> The duty to confront and reprove a brother was deeply rooted in Judaism. Leviticus 19:17, the verse before the command to "love your neighbor as yourself" (cf. Matthew 22:39), requires one to "reprove your neighbor, or you shall incur guilt yourself." The duty to reprove, moreover, must be an act of love. If one allows sin to remain in the community [Church] by refusing to confront one's kin (or doing so out of hate), "you shall incur guilt yourself."[45]

Moreover, Jesus recognized that reconciliation may not be achieved by the efforts of the two parties alone. If this turns out to be the case, then the two disciples should escalate their attempt at reconciliation by taking "one or two other" [believers] to assist them with their reconciliation (Matthew 18:16-17). The taking of "one or two other" disciples to hear and possibly mediate between the two disciples in dispute is anticipatory of the "third step, taking the matter to the community, which required that the offense be confirmed by two or more witnesses, as stipulated by Deut. 19:15" in the *Torah*[46]. If the "one or two" Christians have failed to bring the two conflicting parties together in reconciliation, the Gospel of Matthew records Jesus as saying that the matter in conflict should be brought before the entire church for consideration and mediation (Matthew 18:16-17). Also, the gathered community of the church should hear the matter and render judgment as to the way forward for the two disciples in dispute. The Church can render this judgment because Jesus has given it the power to both "bind"—give a negative ruling against someone or something—or "loose"—give a positive ruling for someone or something (Matthew 18:18 NIV). This is the case because Jesus said, "Truly I tell you, whatever you bind on earth will be bound in heaven, and whatever you loose on earth will be loosed in heaven" (Matthew 18:18 NIV).[47] The Church—the community of disciples—has this authority because whenever they are gathered in Jesus' name [authority], the Son of God is present in their midst to convey his authority to a righteous ruling of the Church (Matthew 18:19-20).[48]

Finally, once the Church has agreed on earth about a matter, it must be accepted as binding upon all disciples. If any disciple refuses to listen and abide by the ruling of the Church, the disciple shall be treated as a "pagan or a tax collector" (Matthew 18:17 NIV). Pagans and tax collectors were seen as the chief sinners and "at the bottom of the moral scale" because of their various forms of ritual, moral, and ethical uncleanness that pious, observant Jews tried to avoid.[49] A Christian who is treated as a pagan and tax collector would be thought of by Matthew's original Semitic audience as being "unredeemed and outside the Christian community" and "cut off in the same way as "cutting" someone "off" from the assembly of Israel."[50] However, the question remains of why such a seemingly extreme view to post-moderns would be the perspective of the Church. New Testament scholar R. T. France gives us insight when he writes,

> The object of the gathering is not to pronounce judgment but to strengthen the pastoral appeal, in the hope that the offender may yet "listen." The offender, faced by the disapproval of the whole local disciple community, ought surely to recognize that this was not just a personal grievance on the part of the initiator. Anyone who is not willing to accept such united testimony may then properly be regarded as no longer a fit member of the community.[51]

It seems implausible that the Church's ruling is not a judgment, contrary to France's assertion, although it true that the whole process of confrontation with a brother and/or sister is—or at least should be—a "pastoral appeal." Nevertheless, France's perspective about the "united testimony" of the Church as the community of brothers and sisters is very persuasive.

Third, Matthew 18:15-30 is significant because Jesus' teaching emphasizes that attempting to resolve conflict with a disputing party in the church is not merely commendable, but also necessary, because disciples are not just members in a religious organization, but members of the family God. Jesus says in his teaching that, "If your brother or sister[52] sins, go and point out their fault, just between the two of you" (Matthew 18:15 NIV). It is important to note that Jesus used the familial designation of "brother or sister" to describe the one who has sinned against the other Christian, which "imports a note of personal care."[53] This familial designation is important to our understanding of the text because it implies that Jesus saw his community of disciples as a spiritual family. On the one hand, the term "brother or sister" conveys how a Christian should perceive another believer who has sinned against them. The sinning disciple should not be viewed by the Christian who has been wronged as an enemy to be hated or an opponent to be conquered, but as a fellow member of the family of God. Jesus' use of the terms 'brother' and 'sister' conveys the implicit message that, just as strong familial bonds should assist natural siblings in overcoming occasional disagreements or incidents of an injured relationship, the knowledge that the sinning disciple is a Christian's spiritual sibling should overrule and/or assist in the same way. It also conveys the understanding to the disciple that has been sinned against that the one who has wronged them is their brother or sister because God is their Father through their faith in Jesus Christ. The victim of wrong and the perpetrator of it in the Church are both sons and daughters of God and, as such, are God's "little ones" that the Father of our Lord Jesus is unwilling "to see perish" (Matthew 15:6, 14).

Although there are many insights that can be gleaned from an analysis of Matthew 18:15-30, these are the most important concluding thoughts that are most pertinent to this project. First, the text reveals that sin against another Christian can lead to conflict that cannot always be resolved between persons of like faith alone. Whenever this occurs, the matter of dispute is no longer a personal matter, but one that demands ecclesiastical concern and intervention. Second, the text reminds us that the one who wrongs us within the Church is a brother or sister, one of God's little ones. This reality, signified in this familial designation, shapes how the perpetrator of wrong is perceived by the Christian and the temperament with which the victim of the wrong should be approached. Finally, Matthew's Gospel shows us that attempts to reconcile with one's sister or brother, individually or through the intervention of another Christian or the entire Church, is an act of love that Christ demands so that the victim may not incur guilt by failing to show mercy, forgiveness, and grace as an imitation of Christ (Matthew 9:13; 18:21, 35).

Conclusion

This chapter began with a quest to determine whether using a CCRT is biblical for use in COGIC because everything that is not rooted in Scripture "is going down" to failure. This project can affirm that using a conflict resolution team is indeed biblical for the following reasons. First, CCRT can be seen as biblical because it follows both Jesus' and Paul's teaching to get other Christians involved, or the entire Church, if necessary, to deal with a wrong within the community of faith. This is also congruent with the truth gleaned from the Wisdom Literature of the Hebrew Bible that affirms that a task is best done in teams. Consequently, a conflict resolution team composed of "spiritual" Christians is another method for the Church to get more persons involved in a dispute who can help polarized parties "overtaken" in the fault of stubbornness find peace and understanding in Christian charity (Galatians 6:1).

Second, a conflict resolution team is a biblical notion of resolving an ecclesiastical dispute because new insights on reconciliation can appear when non-emotionally charged persons enter a conflict with fresh eyes. As previously stated, when Christians make an idol out of their issue in church conflicts—as they often do—they become blinded as to how they are complicit in the fostering of "dissensions," which is sin (Galatians 5:20). In fact, ecclesiastical antagonists can even hide their sinful contention behind the facade of "standing for the truth" or being a pseudo-righteous advocate for others who need them.[54] Consequently, this sin in church conflict prevents conflicting Christians from recognizing opportunities for collaboration and/or compromise when it is needed the most. Scripture recognizes that a group of godly persons tends to make better decisions than just one. Therefore, the Wisdom Writer says, "In the multitude of counselors, there is safety" (Proverbs 11:14). A conflict resolution team brings additional counselors into a congregation with different skill sets that can save it from a destruction of its own making.

Third, a CCRT is a biblical resource for the church because it recognizes the work of the Holy Spirit in two significant ways. On the one hand, the members of the CCRT who have specialized training in church conflict operate in the ministry gift as a "teacher [s]" whose critical knowledge helps mature "the saints" from childish conflicts and "edify the Body" of Christ so that it can do its mission (Ephesians 4:11). On the other, since church disputes are spiritual battles at their core, a CCRT is a ministry and not just a methodology of reconciliation. The ministry of reconciliation performed by this innovative conflict resolution team would make these persons who constitute it anointed peacemaking agents, which is central to our identity as "the children of God." (Matthew 5:9 NIV).

CHAPTER III

[1] C. F. Range Jr., ed., *Church of God in Christ Official Manual* (Memphis: Church of God in Christ Publishing House, 1973), 40-41.

[2] Ibid., 40.

[3] A proper COGIC hermeneutic in the Pentecostal tradition is not fundamentalism but a biblical theology that holds the Bible and the illumination of the Holy Spirit in dialectical tension. The Bible read outside of the Spirit will not produce illumination but will be reduced to the constraints of the reader's reason; claims of the Spirit that ignore or are inconsistent with the Bible are considered "the Spirit of error" and not "the Spirit of truth" (John 16:13; I John 4:6). COGIC holds that the Bible and the Spirit are necessary for proper Biblical interpretation of the Holy Spirit, which "teaches and guides one in all truth" (cf. Range Jr., *Church of God Official Manual*, 46).

[4]. Concerning the Pentecostal churches of his youth in Harlem (New York City), James Baldwin writes, "I have never seen anything to equal the fire and excitement that sometimes, without warning, fill a church causing the church, as Leadbelly and so many others have testified to 'rock'"; cf. James Baldwin, "Down at the Cross," in *James Baldwin: Collected Essays, Tony Morrison*, ed. (New York: Penguin Random House, 1998), 306.

[5] Some dismiss the African American Pentecostal call-and-response songs as theologically deficient because they do not articulate its theology in a lengthy way as the hymnody that the Black Church received from European Protestantism. However, note that these call-and-response shout songs are the most proximate to the slaves' singing found in the spirituals and retain the vocal percussion patterns of African singing. Such critiques by some within the Church are oftentimes rooted in an implicit cultural bias in liturgy and worship that the critic may not directly recognize. Rather than African American Pentecostals being apologetic

for the brevity in songs such as "Everything Going Down but the Word of God," they should praise it because the ancestors were gifted in the ability to say so much by saying little.

[6] I will be using a model of biblical interpretation similar to that used within the Wesleyan tradition, not only because I believe it is a sound model but also because the Holiness Movement, from which COGIC is a theological descendent, shares in this Wesleyan heritage.

[7] I refer to the Old Testament as the Hebrew Bible to recognize that the Old Testament was first the Scripture of Israel.

[8] Traditionally, some have believed that this "teacher" or sage was Solomon because he was a son of David and a notable king who ruled in Jerusalem. In addition, the belief for Solomonic authorship seems plausible at first because the author of Ecclesiastes claims to have great wisdom as the biblical tradition describes Solomon, son of David, to have possessed during his life (I Kings 4:30). The Scripture says, "I have acquired great wisdom, surpassing all who were over Jerusalem before me; and my mind has had great experience of wisdom and knowledge" (Ecclesiastes 1:16 NRSV). Nevertheless, we should note that nowhere in Ecclesiastes does it explicitly state that Solomon wrote this, and we cannot be truly certain that the "king" referred to in this collection of sayings in Ecclesiastes was written by Solomon. Therefore, it seems plausible that Ecclesiastes was written by an "anonymous author" and "not the historical Solomon" as ecclesiastical tradition advocates; cf. C. F. Keil and F. Delitzsch, *Commentary on the Old Testament Volumes 6 Proverbs, Ecclesiastes, Song of Solomon* (Peabody: Hendrickson Publishers, Inc., 1966), 650.

[9] Frank Frick notes that the wisdom of the sage in the Wisdom Literature of the Hebrew Bible emerged from personal observation; cf. Frank S. Frick, *A Journey through the Hebrews Scriptures* (Fort Worth:

Harcourt Brace and Company, 1995), 506.

[10]. Ibid., 488.

[11] Ibid.

[12] Ibid.

[13] Ibid.

[14] One example attests that Paul was absent from his congregation when he said, "Therefore, my beloved, just as you have always obeyed me, not only in my presence, but much more now in my absence, work out your own salvation with fear and trembling" (Philippians 2:12).

[15] It is significant that Paul established churches in the cities by design and not the countryside because Paul's "world does not include the *chora*, the productive countryside"; cf. Wayne A. Meeks, *The First Urban Christians: The Social World of the Apostle Paul* (New Haven and London: Yale University Press, 1983), 9, 75.

[16] Ibid., 16.

[17]. Murphy-O'Connor concurs with this view of the Pauline letters when he writes that, "From a number of points of view Paul's use of letters is best paralleled by that of Epicurus (341-270 BC; Bailey) who 'exhorted, encouraged, gave advice, settled disputes, taught his doctrines, and maintained fellowship through his letters'"; cf. Jerome Murphy-O'Conner, *Paul the Letter-Writer: His World, His Options, His Skill* (Collegeville: The Liturgical Press, 1995), 44.

[18] I contend that it is accurate to see Euodia and Syntche as female coworkers in ministry with Paul and not male because the "Greek names are in the feminine gender" and the "Greek feminine pronouns *'autais* and *haitines* in Phi 4:3, which can only refer back to Euodia and Syntche, require that both names belong to women"; cf. David N. Freedman, ed., *The Anchor Bible Dictionary*, vol. 2 D-G (New York: Double Day, 1992), 670.

[19] The New Testament scholar James D. G. Dunn notes that it is not of extreme significance who is named in Paul's letters and who is not. In the case of the husband-and-wife missionary team Prisca and Aquila, Paul names Prisca before her husband; cf. James D. G. Dunn, *The Theology of Paul the Apostle* (Grand Rapids: William B. Eerdmans Publishing Company, 1998), 587. Dunn argues that this suggests that "she was the more dominant of the two" (cf. Ibid., 587). Dunn also observes that Paul distinguishes other women like Mary, Tryphaena, Tryphosa, and Persis by naming them as hardworking in his letter to the Romans (Ibid., 588).

[20] Richard R. Meilick Jr., *The New American Commentary: An Exegetical and Theological Exposition of Holy Scripture Philippians, Colossians, Philemon,* vol. 32 (Nashville: B and H Publishing Group, 1991), 28, 146.

[21] Fiorenza, *In Memory of Her,* 169.

[22] Meeks notes, concerning I Corinthians, that "it was not from the official letter that Paul heard about the factions, but from members of Chloe's household who happened to come to Ephesus" (cf. Meeks, *The First Urban Christians*, 118). This suggests that there are multiple ways that Paul could have received the news about what was going on in the Philippian congregation.

[23] Evidence for such a claim is found in Paul's statement that he wrote the Corinthian Church a "letter of tears" that proceeded his second letter to the Corinthian congregation contained in the New Testament. The existence of this lost letter can be inferred in II Corinthians 2:3-4, 5:13, 7:8-12, and 10:9-10; cf. David Fredrickson, "'Through Many Tears' (2 Cor. 2:4): Paul's Grieving Letter and the Occasion of 2 Corinthians 2:1-7," Luther's Digital Commons Faculty Publications, https://digitalcommons.luthersem.edu/cgi/viewcontent.cgi?article=1215&context=faculty_articles.

[24] The uncertainty of Paul's release from house arrest can be inferred exegetically in his statements about the possibility to "depart and be with

Christ" in death (Philippians 1:23 NIV).

25 Meeks, *The First Urban Christians*, 142-43.

26 The Philippian congregation probably followed the pattern of the Corinthian congregation, who gathered on the first day of the week before the Lord's Supper; cf. I Corinthians 11:16-20, 16:2; Meeks, *The First Urban Christians*, 142-43. There is evidence from the Lukan writer that this practice was followed in other Pauline churches (Acts 20:7).

27 Ibid., 80.

28 The word "φρονῆτεa" or "*phronete*" can be translated as mind or "understanding"; cf. Joseph H. Thayer, *Thayer's Greek-English Lexicon of the New Testament* (Grand Rapids: Baker Books, 1977), 658.

29 αὐτὸ φρονῆτεa is translated as *auto phronete,* the "same mind," or "to have [the same αὐτὸ] understanding" (cf. Ibid.) Therefore, Paul is asking the Philippian Church to have the same understanding or attitude that Christ had that allowed him to take the way of humility. This understanding would cause conflict to cease in the Philippian congregation.

30 The word "φρονεῖν" or "*phronien*" is translated as "concern" in the New International Version of Philippians 4:10. φρονεῖν can also be translated as "to take thought, have a care, for one" (cf. Ibid.).

31 Fiorenza, *In Memory of Her*, 170.

32 Meilick Jr., *The New American Commentary*, 146.

33 Alfred Poirier, *The Peace-Making Pastor: A Biblical Guide to Resolving Church Conflict* (Grand Rapids: Baker Books, 2006), X.

34 Meilick concurs with Paul's attempt to get the whole church involved in the dispute between Euodia and Syntche when he wrote that their conflict was "divisive enough to cause the church to write to Paul about it; the entire church was asked to intercede on behalf of these women" (Ibid.).

[35] I strongly disagree with New Testament scholar R. T. France that the nature of the sin discussed in Matthew 18 could not include a dispute between two Christians who would speak of the sin as a "grievance" or that conflict resolution would be inappropriate; cf. R. T. France, *The New International Commentary on the New Testament: The Gospel of Matthew* (Grand Rapids and Cambridge: William B. Eerdmans Publishing Company, 2007), 693. It may be reasonable to assert that a discussion of a grievance and/or dispute between two Christians is an indirect concern, but to say it is not a concern at all ignores the fact that sin not only breaks our fellowship with God but also damages our relationships with other people and the entire Church (Isaiah 59:2).

[36] The Apostle Paul asserts that "hatred, contentions, jealousies, outburst of wrath, selfish ambitions, dissensions" are "works of the flesh" that are sins (Galatians 5:20). We know this to be the case because Paul maintains that "those who practice such things will not inherit the kingdom of God" (Galatians 5:21). It is rare to find examples of church conflicts that lack these "works of the flesh" mentioned by the sainted apostle.

[37] The word "ἐκκλησία" or "church," used in Matthew 16:17, has "in view the church universal," and Matthew 16:15 "refers to the local community," as it does in most of the other occurrences of the term in the NT; cf. R. Alan Culpepper, *Matthew: A Commentary* (Louisville: Westminster John Knox Press, 2021), 346; and Craig L. Blomberg, *The New American Commentary: An Exegetical and Theological Exposition of Holy Scripture Matthew,* vol. 22 (Nashville: B and H Publishing Company, 1992), 33.

[38] Culpepper, *Matthew,* 23.

[39] William H. Willimon, *Preaching about Conflict in the Local Church* (Philadelphia: The Westminster Press, 1987), 44.

[40] Culpepper, *Matthew,* 19.

[41] The presentation of Jesus as teacher guiding his community is a Semitic nuance that should not be overlooked. It has long been noted by many

scholars that Matthew's Gospel is the most Jewish of all the Gospels and that its principal audiences are those of a Semitic background (cf. Ibid., 3). Culpepper argues that "Matthew's community was composed of Jews who believed that Jesus was the Messiah of Israel and continued to be law-observant Jews" (cf. Ibid., 26). Keener concurs in that he sees the principal audience as "a largely Jewish ideal audience who will understand many of his allusions"; cf. Craig S. Keener, *A Commentary on the Gospel of Matthew* (Grand Rapids and Cambridge: William B. Eerdmans Publishing Company, 1999), 45. The Jewishness of Matthew's Gospel is also shown in that the numerous Scriptural citations suggest that the Matthean writer "could read the Scriptures in their original language" and was not totally dependent on the Septuagint (cf. Ibid., 9). Finally, the Gospel of Matthew's Jewish orientation is shown in how the author re-Judaizes his sources and his portrayal of Jesus himself (cf. Ibid., 10,13, 45-46); Blomberg, *The New American Commentary*, 27.

[42] Keener, *Commentary*, 13.

[43] Matthew 18:15 merely says that a brother has sinned against another; it doesn't specify the sin. I strongly disagree with New Testament scholar R. T. France that the nature of the sin discussed in Matthew 18 could not include a dispute between two Christians, which would speak of the sin as a "grievance" or that conflict resolution would be inappropriate; cf. France, *The Gospel of Matthew*, 693. It may be reasonable to assert that a discussion of a grievance and/or dispute between two Christians is an indirect concern, but to say it is not a concern at all ignores the fact that sin not only breaks our fellowship with God but also damages our relationships with other people and the entire Church (Isaiah 59:2).

[44] Culpepper, *Matthew*, 345.

[45] Ibid.

[46] Ibid., 346.

[47] Culpepper notes that the "authority conferred upon the church in

matters of discipline, forgiveness or banishment is seemingly absolute" (cf. Ibid., 348). He also noted that the "Greek verb is a future periphrasatic perfect passive participle; literally, "It shall have been bound/loosed"—that is, eternally so (cf. Ibid.). New Testament scholar Craig L. Blomberg asserts that "the church's loosing and binding—forgiving or refusing to forgive—carries the very authority of God" (cf. Blomberg, *The New American Commentary*, 280).

[48] The Jewish rabbis believed that the *'Shekinah*—the glory of God that was once present in the temple in the Holy of Holies— "was present wherever the law was studied, whether it be in a group of ten, where there only two, or even where there was only one righteous person" (cf. Culpepper, *Matthew*, 348). Matthew projects the imagery of the *'Shekinah* to the post-resurrected "presence of Jesus" whenever "the faithful are gathered 'in my name'" (cf. Ibid.).

[49] Tax collectors were considered sinners because they charged interest on their taxes and were frequently around Gentiles [pagans], who were perceived as sexually immoral, ritually impure due to their partaking of non-kosher foods and drink offered to idols, and worshippers of gods that were really demons (cf. Ibid., 347; Deuteronomy 23:19; I Corinthians 10:20; France, *The Gospel of Matthew*, 694).

[50] Blomberg, *The New American Commentary*, 279.

[51] France, *The Gospel of Matthew*, 693. Keener affirms my view that "binding" and "loosing" refer to the judicial authority of gathered Christians to decide cases based on God's law. Thus, most scholars recognize that this passage applies to church discipline; Keener, *Commentary*, 455.

[52] The New Testament Greek in this Matthean passage only refers to the offending Christian as "brother" and not sister, but it is obvious Christians of either gender can sin against another (Ibid., 344). Consequently, many modern translations have added both "brother" and "sister" in their rendering of this passage, such as in the New International Version. The

New Revised Standard Version, in its commitment to gender inclusivity, attempted to resolve this problem by translating verse 15 as "another member of the church sins against you" (Matthew 18:15 NRSV). The problem with the NRSV translation is that removing the familial designation of "brother" for the goal of gender inclusivity creates the problem of erasing how the sinning Christian should be viewed by the other believer who is wronged. Therefore, it is more prudent to let the original, literal rendering remain and see the term "brother" as "inclusive" (Ibid., 344).

[53] France, *The Gospel of Matthew,* 691.

[54] An antagonist who claims to be "standing for the truth" often falls into the role of "the activist," who makes their issues more important than the harmony of the institution of the local church to which they are a part; cf. Kenneth Haugk, *Antagonist in the Church: How to Identify and Deal with Destructive Conflict* (Minneapolis: Augsburg Publishing House, 1988), 38.

CHAPTER FOUR

"I WILL MAKE THE DARKNESS LIGHT"

"I will make the darkness light before thee,

What is wrong I'll make it right before thee,

All thy battles I will fight before thee,

And the high place I'll bring down." [1]

Congregational conflict is an overwhelming darkness that hides the light of a local church's Christian witness and exposes all that is wrong with human nature. Consequently, churches in this horrible state face a "high place" of division, discord, and death of common bonds within the congregation and desperately need the light of peace to return to their midst. This chapter will meet the challenge of congregational disputes by providing a solution to this perplexing problem. This will be accomplished in the following ways. First, this chapter will define each member of the CCRT and why their presence is essential to the team as an agent of reconciliation. This chapter will also clearly define the purpose of the CCRT within the denomination. Finally, the chapter will explain the site visit operational procedure of CCRTs at the congregations where they have been deployed.

The Members of the CCRT

The members of the CCRT proposed by this project should consist of the following: a clinical counselor, a prayer warrior, an ordained elder with a minimum of 10 years of pastoral experience, and a woman in ministry. The first proposed member of the CCRT should be a clinical counselor—preferably a psychiatrist or psychologist—who can look at a church dispute with clinical eyes. Traditionally, Pentecostals—with a few exceptions—have been reluctant to use clinical resources to assist their members and their churches. This disposition towards clinicians among Pentecostals has two significant causes. On the one hand, Pentecostals have a high view of prayer and God's ability to supernaturally intervene in the lives of Christians and particularly the local church through it.[2] Consequently, some within COGIC still equate using clinical resources with a lack of faith in God's power to supernaturally deliver a person or church without the use of human tools.[3] Fortunately, this minority within the COGIC constituency is steadily decreasing because of the rising educational level of many members of the denomination and the increasing visibility of some COGIC clinical counselors, psychiatrist, and psychologist among the ranks of the faithful. However, old beliefs—no matter how incongruent with Scripture and reason—resist death with great vigor. On the other hand, many Pentecostals—COGIC in particular—do not commonly use clinical resources because they believe that their congregational budget cannot afford them and/or they may not be knowledgeable as to where to find them within their community.[4] The inability of a COGIC congregation to afford clinical resources may not be an excuse, since most American congregations have

50 or fewer members; this is exactly why the denomination should retain its own clinical resources to eliminate this problem.

Fortunately, this minority within the COGIC constituency is steadily decreasing due to the rising educational levels of many members of the denomination combined with the increasing visibility of some COGIC clinical counselors, psychiatrists, and psychologists among the ranks of the faithful. When it comes to old beliefs—no matter how incongruent with Scripture and reason they may be—this minority resist death with great vigor. On the other hand, many Pentecostals—COGIC Pentecostals in particular—do not commonly use clinical resources because they believe that their congregational budgets cannot afford them, or they may not be knowledgeable as to where to find them within their communities.[5] A COGIC congregation's inability to afford clinical resources may not be an excuse, as most American congregations are 50 members or less. This is exactly why the denomination should retain its own clinical resources.

Nevertheless, the clinical lens is essential for analyzing destructive church conflicts for multiple reasons. First, it is beneficial to have a psychiatrist, psychologist, or a clinical counselor apply a psycho-social lens to holistically analyze church conflicts in our COGIC congregations. The assertion that clinical and mental health counselors are necessary for resolving church conflicts does not deny the fact that disputes within churches are spiritual battles. To the contrary, what we assert in this project is that we need the professional insights of clinical and mental health counselors, as church conflicts are more than spiritual battles.

Church conflicts entail the perception and misperception of issues; the receiving, conveying, and interpretation of physical and verbal communication; and anxiety from persons and factions within a congregation whose members perceive some form of change as threatening them. To shrug off a dispute within a congregation as merely a demonic attack on a local church is simply not accurate and fails to recognize the human element that is inherent in all disputes. Consequently, using the clinical lens in COGIC CRT does not stop or discourage prayer in a church conflict; however, it does provide additional information so that the local church knows all the factors involved in the dispute and thus know exactly what to pray about.

It is also essential to have clinical resources for congregations in conflict, such as psychiatrist or psychologist, because some hard-core antagonists in church disputes are indeed "psychotic—out of touch with reality."[6] Another party involved in a church conflict is the "major antagonist," who has "a character or personality disorder" that prevents them from behaving rationally.[7] Unfortunately, both types of antagonists are known for making "insatiable demands" to the church and/or its leadership, which disrupt the peace of the congregation. Indeed, any attempt at conflict resolution with these types of persons without clinical knowledge will ultimately fail because the uninformed mediators will engage these antagonists as if they are normal persons. Prayer and reasoning alone are often inadequate in church conflict if someone who has a mental illness is the one generating it, as it needs to be treated as other illnesses requiring the care of a medical provider. Jessica Brown rightly notes that we must treat mental illness as all other illnesses by having the saints "pray, and then we seek the help and support we need" from a qualified clinician.[8] Consequently, someone is needed who can accurately determine whether a congregational dispute is birthed out of an honest disagreement or whether it is rooted in mental disorders that surprisingly hide well in ecclesiastical settings in both the pulpit and the pew.[9]

Also, having a psychiatrist, psychologist, and/or clinical counselor is critical for dealing with congregational disputes, as some church conflicts are the result of cognitive decline in aging pastors with some form of dementia or Alzheimer's disease. Many pastors are seniors and are at least theoretically vulnerable to some form of cognitive decline due to aging, but some unfortunately suffer from severe forms of this decline, such as dementia and/or Alzheimer's disease. Pastors who suffer from these severe types of cognitive decline lose their "sense of unadulterated judgement, and planning as well as organizing mental capacity," which are essential basic skill sets for the Christian pastorate.[10] Moreover, pastors with Alzheimer's or dementia may experience radical change in their moods or personalities whereby they may become "very shy" and withdraw from public church functions, or they may become very "harsh" in their treatment of congregants because "they cannot control their mood."[11] The congregations that such pastors lead will find themselves emotionally torn by the ethical dilemmas of being compassionate and loyal toward their pastors—who most likely served them well in the past—as well as the need to have competent spiritual leaders to care for their local churches, feed the, and lead them in the present.

Eventually, conflict will arise within the congregation when a pastor in cognitive decline is leading it, as the local church must have a pastor who can make prudent decisions, plan worship, lead the church as its chief executive officer, and not run off or embarrass the congregation because they cannot control their mood in both public and private. Therefore, frustration will boil over in a COGIC church that has a dementia- or Alzheimer's-inflicted pastor who has become incapacitated due to their illness. This is the case because members may request ecclesiastical intervention to remove such a pastor to protect the best interests of the church only to discover that the jurisdictional bishop lacks the constitutional authority to do such on these grounds alone.[12] In this project, we assert that a mental health clinician would be able to recognize cognitive decline in the pastor and assist the congregation in convincing the family and pastor to assume an emeritus status for the good of both the pastor and the church they have charge of. This will not be an easy endeavor because many pastors lack an adequate pastoral retirement, and their spouses and families may benefit both politically and financially from the pastors' retaining their pastoral charge even when they are in cognitive decline.

Second, in this project, we assert that a gifted prayer warrior should be a member of the CCRT.[13] The term "prayer warrior" should be defined at this point in the project because it is a designation that may not be understood beyond the borders of COGIC and/or the Pentecostal Tradition. Prayer warriors are known in the COGIC denomination for two qualities. On the one hand, prayer warriors are deeply pious Christians who spend many hours in prayer on a regular basis—both privately and publicly—and lead congregations and bands of Christians in corporate prayer within COGIC. Also, most COGIC ecclesiastical jurisdictions have "prayer warriors" who are part of their official jurisdictional staff. These individuals are so disciplined and habitual in their practice of prayer that they are said to have "the spirit of prayer" and labor daily in the "prayer ministry."[14]

Mother E. J. Dabney

The late Mother Elizabeth Juanita Dabney is a famous example of a COGIC prayer warrior who was the sainted cofounder and first lady of the Garden of Prayer Church of God in Christ in Philadelphia, Pennsylvania. She was the wife of the late Bishop Benjamin H. Dabney.[15] This pious woman was so disciplined and habitual in her prayer ministry that she made and kept a vow to God to pray every day at "nine o'clock am sharp" accompanied by three years of fasting "seventy-two hours each week."[16] Mother Dabney claimed that this three-year consecration culminated in her receiving a powerful "anointing" that led to the growth of her church and a miraculous prayer ministry that touched thousands all over the world, crossing racial and denominational lines until her death in 1967.[17] Her autobiographical book *What It Means to Pray Through* briefly reflects on the prayer ministry of another prayer warrior and one of Dabney's mentors, Mother Harriet M. Ways. She was the founder and first church mother of the historic Holy Temple Church of God in Christ, Inc., in Philadelphia, Pennsylvania. She was also the second supervisor of women in the state of Pennsylvania, whom Mother Dabney called the "Queen of Prayer."[18] This was the case because Supervisor Harriet M. Ways led a group of sainted women to set times of habitual prayer to raise the morale of struggling churches within the state of Pennsylvania when many were struggling both spiritually and economically during the Great Depression of the twentieth century.[19] Mother Dabney recollected that, "She [Mother Harriet M. Ways] called the praying women together and prayed two days monthly in each church…She sent out a prayer-call to all prayer warriors who each morning from seven until eight who met the Lord in prayer. Some preferred from eight until nine, therefore we had 'Two Watches,' She prayed until the Lord lifted the band of depression and sent the people work."[20]

On the other, prayer warriors in COGIC are not known as people who merely pray but rather as powerful individuals whose prayers are known to get results signified by numerous conversions, baptisms in the Holy Spirit, deliverance from spiritual bondage, physical healings, and church renewal. Bishop C. H. Mason (1864-1961), the first senior bishop, chief apostle, and illustrious founder of the Church of God in Christ, Inc., was thought of as such an individual. Bishop C. H. Mason's devotion to the practice of prayer was rooted in the piety that Mason saw demonstrated by former African American slaves, most importantly his mother Elizabeth

(Eliza) Mason. Mason's daughter once commented that, "While he [Mason] was growing up, he often prayed with his mother and asked God to give him the same religion he saw manifested in his mother and former slaves."[21]

Bishop Charles H. Mason

The ministry of Bishop C. H. Mason is now legendary in the recollections of his spiritual descendants due to the numerus miracles attributed to his prayer ministry until his death in 1961. Bishop Mason's prayer ministry was so powerful that it impacted thousands, who sought to improve their own devotional lives as a result. The late Bishop Otha M. Kelly, the former first assistant presiding bishop and an early pastor of the Kelly Temple Church of God in Christ in the village of Harlem New York, said, "Bishop Mason didn't spend too much time in prayer at night. But in the morning, he spent two or three hours every day on his knees. When he got tired praying on his knees, he takes the pillow off the bed, sit down on it and keep on praying. His prayer life taught me what God can do with a man if he'll learn how to pray and wait on God for the answers."[22]

The denomination's first chief apostle is reported to have prayed upon the ground during a violent storm in a church meeting that threatened the lives of Bishop Mason and the congregants. As fear gripped many within this particular meeting, Bishop Mason rose from his knees in prayer and "cried unto the Lord to send peace and rebuke the storm."[23] Reportedly, the storm ceased "immediately," and the lives of the congregants and Bishop Mason were spared.[24] Afterward, a "very wicked man [who] was in the service" who witnessed "God almighty handiwork in that place he ran forward and fell at Bishop Mason's feet, and cried, "It's enough," and the Lord saved his soul."[25] Regardless of whether a person believes this account of Bishop Mason to be an embellished story or outright fiction is secondary to the fact that thousands believed in him as a prayer warrior, and this belief directly affected their personal piety.

In addition, Bishop Mason is said to have "prevailed with the Lord" so much so that God would put the gifting of a powerful prayer ministry "upon some of his children in the Gospel" within COGIC.[26] Prayer Warriors such as Mother E. J. Dabney (1915-1967)—and more recently the late Mother Elsie Shaw—often stated that they, too, received and coveted "the spirit of prayer like unto his [Bishop Mason]," and many believed that they indeed did.[27] Consequently, thousands of persons attributed their physical healings to Mother Dabney's prayers so much so that the original Garden of Prayer COGIC sanctuary was adorned—not only with a pipe organ and stained glass windows—but crutches, canes, and other items associated with sickness leaved behind by those who claimed they had been healed.[28]

Mother Elsie Shaw - COGIC Prayer Warrior

However, the question remains why would a prayer warrior be fitting member of a CCRT? On the one hand, having a prayer warrior to go to congregations in crisis is congruent with COGIC's historic practice because prayer was seen as a powerful tool of conflict resolution. Bishop Charles H. Mason frequently used corporate prayer meetings as a tool for conflict resolution in the early years of the denomination. The late Mother Lillian Brooks Coffey (1891-1964), who served as COGIC's second general supervisor of women, recounts this fact in her tribute at Bishop Mason's funeral in 1961. She said, "I have seen him [Bishop Mason] go in where there was Great Confusion and Pray for hours and hours. When he got up, the trouble was ALL OVER!"[29]

Mother L. B. Coffey

A known prayer warrior's presence would cause a surge in morale for a conflict-battered congregation, as COGIC adherents expect a positive change to occur when prayer warriors arrive. This is because such a belief is congruent with the theology and historical narratives of COGIC. Therefore, the late Bishop Samuel Kelsey (1898-1993) pleaded with Mother Dabney's husband to allow her to be sent to him in the early years of his church planting in Washington, D.C., after he led an unsuccessful tent meeting.[30] Certainly, the morale of Bishop Kelsey and his members increased when Mother Dabney arrived in Washington, D.C., due to her national reputation for supernatural signs following her ministry. Fortunately, Bishop Kelsey's confidence in Mother Dabney's prayer ministry was not misplaced, as her labor in prayer under the tent for two weeks led to 95 persons being converted and the growth of what would later become the historic Kelsey Temple Church of God in Christ.[31] Therefore, in this instance, the pastor and congregation perceived the presence and intercession of a prayer warrior as being linked to church renewal. In this project, we are certain that contemporary COGIC adherents would think the same because such a notion is deeply imbedded in the denomination's history and tradition. Mother Dabney articulated this view when she talked about the prayer revivals conducted in the "old camp meeting" or "protracted meeting" of former years.[32] She says, "Both men and women made it their business to assemble together in cottage meetings or the church house. They corrected mistakes and repented for whatever they had in their hearts that displeased God and their fellow workers. When they adjusted matters and conditions, it changed the very atmosphere in the community, in the home and the church."[33]

Prayer meetings that prayer warriors lead created an atmosphere for the membership to repent and to get out of their hearts the things that displease God and their fellow members, which led to a change in the church's atmosphere.

Also, prayer warriors ought to be part of a COGIC conflict resolution team because church conflicts are at its heart—spiritual battles for the soul of a congregation—and not just personality clashes on display. It is interesting that Mother Dabney's autobiographical account illustrates incidents of church conflict in the pioneering years of Garden of Prayer COGIC as battles against Satan. She describes "hypocrites and pretenders" in the church as the devil's "angels"; they could be found "seated on the front pews in the church."[34] She says, "By this time many of our members had learned to contact God in prayer; they were ready for the battle. The Lord sent shower after shower of blessings upon us, and the devil sent this woman from place to place, warning the people not to come there [the church]."

It is noteworthy that Mother Dabney did think that the woman was responsible for her actions, but she still held to the belief that the ultimate source of conflict that "the woman" generated was "the devil."[35] This view of church conflict is congruent with COGIC theology because we believe that destructive conflict in churches is rooted in Satan's desire to stifle or halt the Church's mission of evangelism, discipleship, and ministry to its community. Mother Dabney notes that she did not use earthly means to overcome the opposition from the woman; to the contrary, "prayer defeated her [the antagonist]." Consequently, prayer is seen as an effective tool of spiritual warfare that is not given adequate attention in many conflict resolution approaches for churches.

Earlier in this chapter, we mentioned that church conflict cannot be completely reduced to just spiritual warfare to deny the human element and over-spiritualize congregational conflict, which is a common tendency within the Pentecostal Tradition. However, we strongly deny that church conflict can be reduced to only poor interpersonal relations between human beings within the congregation as well. The truth of the matter is that church conflicts are both manifestations of both humanity and the supernatural that should be observed in dialectical tension to gain an accurate view of a congregation's problem. Consequently, a prayer warrior needs to intercede on behalf of the congregation and lead the congregation in the act of intercession while training in conflict resolution is conducted, preaching is done, and mediation between disputing factions within a church takes place. This is the case because without Christ and his power, nothing positive can be accomplished to resolve a church conflict. In fact, the first causality in a church dispute is usually prayer (John 15:5). Therefore, the denomination should deploy prayerful individuals to troubled congregations to fight against the dark, demonic forces that manipulate human fallenness to divide and destroy local churches. This should be done until the members regain the ability to say yes to God.[36]

The third member of the proposed CCRT should be a seasoned ordained elder who has pastored a COGIC congregation for a minimum of ten years and has formal training in conflict resolution. The reason for this requirement is twofold. On the one hand, it is usually the case that someone who has held a pastoral charge successfully for at least ten years is not a ministerial novice and has a reasonable degree of practical wisdom. This practical wisdom that an experienced elder possesses allows this CCRT member to weave his experience in pastoral leadership, denominational polity, engaging church boards and auxiliaries, and navigating past church disputes to give wise advisement to a congregation and pastor in turmoil in consultation with the other team members. Indeed, much about pastoring is caught in the process of congregational interactions rather than being taught in a seminary classroom or read in a book on organizational leadership. Unfortunately, many church conflicts erupt in congregations because the local pastor is immature and/or inexperienced, and sometimes corrupt in how they exercise their pastoral authority, or they lack the insight to respond properly to the informal power of an influential person they pastor within his local church. An ordained elder who is a veteran pastor can potentially discern if this is the case in a congregational conflict because not only are they an ordained elders but also, they supervise these elders in their local church and are familiar with the failures of their colleagues in their sacred vocation.

A CCRT member who is an ordained elder with the attribute of practical wisdom gained from at least a decade of pastoral ministry makes it difficult for the pastor and congregation to dismiss their advisement and critiques. The truth is, pastors and congregations in conflict are not always open to the truth that will make them free from the divisions in their midst. It is human nature to believe that a given situation is unique and that only the persons involved in the conflict truly understand the challenge that the congregation faces in it. Nevertheless, this perception—although real in the minds of those who think them—are seldom true. An ordained elder with a minimum of a decade of experience can affirm through their past experiences that this is not the case.

The fourth proposed member of COGIC's conflict resolution team should be a male or female who is a gifted preacher. In this project, we view preaching as an indispensable tool for helping to navigate and combat congregational conflict for the following reasons. First, preaching reminds the congregation of their God-ordained mission as a gathered community that they have been distracted from amid their conflict. When churches with conflict egos undermine evangelism, disrespect becomes the norm instead of discipleship, and those who are called to lead mismanage the ministry. A gifted minister who can preach with passionate precision on the mission of the Church as articulated in the Great Commission after it has been neglected during a local church's disputes can make preaching itself "a major component in conflict resolution" (Matthew 28:19-20; Mark 16:15; Luke 24:47-49; Acts 1:8).[37] William H. Willimon's insightful observation highlights the relationship among an understanding of the Church's mission, conflict, and preaching. He says,

> One fundamental reason why congregations are plagued with conflict is that there is no consensus about the purpose and nature of the church.... Preaching, as a major source of Christian identity, is the chief opportunity for reiterating the stories, values, and visions that make a congregation Christian. Through this process the community gathers and focuses itself, celebrates it common goals, and underscores its mission. All of this is to suggest that much of our preaching, while not specifically related to solving a particular

> conflict within the congregation, is essential preparation for the Christian resolution of conflicts when they occur. A congregation that has no center, no general consensus about the direction of the church, is ill equipped to handle crisis. Thus, preaching that occurs in a congregation, week in and week out, is a major component in conflict resolution.[38]

On the other hand, a gifted preacher can assist in conflict resolution because anointed preaching can move the congregation into another frame of mind, where they can be edified and moved to corporate repentance. This is the case because "words are more powerful than we realize," as a preacher's "sermon can create an atmosphere for everything that occurs within a church," as Alphonetta Wines noted.[39] Dr. James Forbes, the former pastor of the Riverside Church, gives us the reason why preaching can change a local church's atmosphere. He says that this is the case because "preaching" is bearing witness to the resurrecting power of God, which extends itself into the regions of death, so that the new life in Christ breaks forth in all dimensions of the created order."[40] The CCRT who comes into a congregation in conflict has come into "the regions of death" because fellowship and common bonds have been broken and in some cases have died, and a high place of division has been set up among the people. Nevertheless, the preacher on the CCRT is present on the team because they must preach through this ecclesiastical death until the "new life in Christ breaks forth in all dimensions" into the congregation and harmony is restored.

However, it is not just any words or sermon that has this effect: what is needed are words or sermons whose content and agent is Holy Spirit anointed. Consequently, a gifted preacher—in the Pentecostal understanding—is not just someone who is endowed with eloquent oratory in their sermons. (Many powerful Pentecostal preachers were not refined in their styles of speech or did not follow the conventions of homiletics due to a lack of formal seminary training.) To the contrary, a gifted preacher is one who is endowed with the Holy Spirit's manifested presence, which causes hearts to be converted and minds to change to become conducive to the will of God. This criterion alone is how a preacher is truly called gifted because they have received power from the one who is the perfect gift: the glorious third person of the Trinity. Therefore Dr. Forbes' words are so pertinent to us when we consider congregational conflict as a form of ecclesiastical death. He says, "Preachers who have not been anointed cannot cope with the death of these times- and there are different kinds of death. We all have a job that cannot be done with just a cute homily, with three points and a poem. Our task is going to take more than that!"[41]

Finally, the fifth member of the CCRT should be composed of a seasoned female deaconess or evangelist missionary. The presence of a female in ministry in the CCRT is imperative to mediating conflicts in COGIC congregations. This is the case because women make up the largest demographic of our church despite not being ordained members of the presbytery.[42] In addition, women in COGIC congregations may lack co-equal authority with their pastors, but they sometimes hold more congregational influence than the pastor does in that they are subject to denominational polity. This is the case because women in COGIC congregations are often matriarchs of families in local churches. Also, the pastor may hold the power of the pulpit, but in many cases, the women of a COGIC congregation holds the power of the purse. This is true because COGIC women are usually the major fundraisers in church programs, so pastors are dependent on them. In fact, even the denomination's first bank account was made possible in 1917 by a sizable deposit of $168.50 by the COGIC Department of Women and not the general church, which male ordained elders and bishops lead.[43] Finally, many COGIC women are hugely influential because some possess tremendous charismatic gifting and spiritual power that may surpass that of the senior pastor despite not having ordination credentials. Therefore, an all-male CCRT would probably be blind to how gender influences issues of power in church disputes.

The Purpose of the COGIC Conflict Resolution Team

The purpose of this innovative approach toward conflicts in COGIC churches would be to assist pastors and churches in understanding and resolving destructive church conflict within their midst. The CCRT would accomplish this goal by doing four things. First, the CCRT would elevate the pastor and congregation above their church conflict by conducting spiritual practices (e.g., revival meetings, prayer meetings, and fasting) in the Holiness-Pentecostal Tradition that foster greater spirituality, honest introspection, and congregational cohesion. The goal of this first phase of the CCRT is to recreate a spiritual environment within the congregation so that the church membership can become open to the conflict resolution process and to the loving conviction of the Holy Spirit, which calls them to a state of corporate repentance. This spiritual goal is essential because it is the foundation, which the CCRT will build upon in their work. Second, the CCRT will educate COGIC pastors and church members on the nature and types of congregational conflict through workshops and consultations, both in an individual and in a corporate manner as needed. As stated earlier, most COGIC clergy and laity have experience with church conflict, but few have informed knowledge on how it starts and how to stop it. The training that the CCRT would give to the congregations would include informative tools for seeing their disputes for what they are so that they can resolve them. Third, the denominational conflict team will conclude their work by mediating between conflicting parties within a COGIC congregation to identify the issues of contention and to work towards a solution. Fourth, the jurisdictional prelate of the COGIC congregation would receive a detailed report from the conflict resolution team before their departure concerning the church they were sent to assist.

The Explanation of the Site Visit Procedure by the CCRT

Details about how the COGIC resolution team will operate shall be the following. First, the conflict resolution team will visit the church site as visitors and worshippers on a Sunday morning to observe the congregation before their intervention takes place.

It is preferable that this visit take place when the senior pastor is delivering the weekly sermon and not an associate minister or an evangelist missionary. The date of the arrival of the CCRT should be generally known to the leadership of the church, but not the specific date so that the CCRT can accurately observe the congregational dynamics in its natural state. The CCRT should take care to refrain from engaging the pastor or the congregants of the local church in the Sunday worship service that they attend as visitors and worshippers when they make the site visit. This disciplined approach should be maintained because pastors and congregations in conflict often attempt to appear that all is well in a local church and that things are not as bad as it has been reported to outsiders. However, a false image of a local church that the pastor, members of the congregation, or both give to the CCRT is not helpful to the team or to the congregation in the end. In addition, a premature conversation with the pastor or the congregation can give the CCRT a distorted view of the local church situation.

Second, the CCRT should meet with the pastor, deacons, church mother, trustee board, and remainder of the congregation on a mid-week service night—preferably on the Tuesday after the Sunday morning visit—on a special call meeting of the congregation. The issues of the congregation should not be discussed in this call meeting with the pastor and/or the congregation. Instead, the purpose of this call meeting should be twofold. First, the call meeting should introduce the congregational members to the CCRT in general. Second, the call meeting should introduce the members of the local church to the specific expertise of each team member. After the CCRT has introduced themselves to the members of the church site for their intervention, the pastor should dismiss the congregation with prayer and a benediction.

Third, the CCRT shall begin their intervention with a revival that should be conducted for three days to raise the spiritual conscience of the congregation and move them to corporate repentance. The revival conducted via the CCRT should have two parts. The CCRT prayer warrior will lead the congregation in corporate prayer for three nights from 6:30-8:00 p.m. in the sanctuary. This will be the first part of the revival to alter the church's site's spiritual climate. The jurisdictional prelate and the CCRT will require that the entire congregation—especially the leadership—attend the prayer meetings in their entirety to participate in the future negotiations. No persons will be allowed to speak and/or participate in the negotiations without attending each night of the prayer services. The prayer warrior can conduct the prayer meeting according to the leading of the Holy Spirit. Nevertheless, three prayer focuses must be followed for each night:

Wednesday-	Prayer for Repentance and Church Renewal
Thursday-	Prayer for Unity
Friday-	Prayer for the Resolution of Issues

The second part of the revival will be a three-night church service that culminates in preaching by a male or female evangelist. The evangelist should be gifted at preaching souls to conversion, the baptism of the Holy Spirit, and the ability to move the saints to a more spiritual state of mind. The evangelist should end their final service on the following Sunday after the arrival of the CCRT. The spiritual climate should hopefully improve after the three nights of prayer and preaching to move forward with the other aspects of the conflict resolution.

The fourth phase of the CCRT intervention is to provide critical training that will educate the pastor and congregation on the nature of church conflicts. This knowledge is critical because unless a pastor and congregation understand how church conflicts work and how they enable them, they will be trapped in endless cycles of contention that will ultimately consume the congregation's health and resources. These are the following training topics that the CCRT will provide to the pastor and its membership at the church site:

Seminar I	Pastoral and Auxiliary Leaders Transitions and Church Conflict
Seminar II	Ecological Shifts That Affect Local Church and Increase Corporate Anxiety
Seminar III	Leaping Before Learning: Moving Too Quickly to Implement Rapid Congregational Change
Seminar IV	Mental Disorders in Church Conflict
Seminar V	The Importance of Effective Collaboration, Compromise, and Communication to Church Leaders and Congregation in Vision Creation and Implementation
Seminar VI	The Proper Stewardship of Influence in the Local Church to Maximize the Common Good

Seminar VII It's All Our Business: The Congregation's Corporate Responsibility to Maintain Church Health

The seven training seminars that the CCRT shall conduct in its church site can be taught over a three-day period—preferably Tuesday, Wednesday, and Thursday nights—or on a two-day period, such as on a Friday and Saturday. The CCRT will consult with the pastor and the church leaders to determine which format would be congruent for the congregation to which they are sent. Also, it is highly recommended that the training seminars be conducted in a retreat format. This can occur in two ways. Either the members and the pastor can be taken out of the church site in a neutral setting, if possible, for the training, or the training can be conducted in the church site's sanctuary or educational facilities with refreshments or food served so that there is time for fellowship to foster positive congregational interaction.

The fifth act of intervention of the CCRT is a day of mediation to discuss the matter of dispute and to get the conflicting parties to speak, listen, collaborate, and compromise if necessary to find a suitable solution for all of those involved. This part of the CCRT may take a day or two, but it must be done considering the training that has been provided that should inform the discussions of all involved. This day of mediation should begin with a thirty-minute prayer session that the prayer warrior completes before discussions occur with the conflicting parties in the congregation.

The sixth and final act of the CCRT's intervention is to present the agreed-upon solution that emerged through the process of mediation to the congregation. Presumably, everyone in the congregation should accept the agreed-upon solution if the pastor and all the influential members publicly express their willingness to abide by the decision reached through the process of mediation. Afterward, the CCRT should depart the church site and send a summary of their findings and recommendation to the jurisdictional prelate of which the church is a part.

The evaluation of the CCRT will be made possible through the cooperation of two jurisdictional prelates within the Church of God in Christ, Inc. They will identify a congregation in conflict within their jurisdiction and implement a proto-CCRT in the manner described within this dissertation project. The tool for evaluation will be a before-and-after questionnaire given to the congregation before and after the CCRT's intervention. The answers on this questionnaire coupled with a period of observation by the jurisdictional prelate will help with determining if the congregational climate has improved or remains poor.

CHAPTER FOUR

[1] Charles Price Jones, "I Will Make the Darkness Light," in Church of God in Christ Hymnal, (Memphis: Church of God in Christ Publishing Board, 1982), 402.

[2] The Pentecostal tradition as it emerged in the early twentieth century did not believe prayer was magic, but it did hold that "prayer could bend nature to one's interest"; cf. Grant Whacker, Heaven Below: Early Pentecostals and American Culture (Cambridge: Harvard University Press, 2001), 24. Therefore, nothing was considered beyond the reach of the petitioner if they simply prevailed in prayer. Sometimes these notions of prayer did not consider the sovereignty of God, despite some of its positive aspects.

[3] Dawn E. Davis maintains in her doctoral dissertation "Strong Black Women, Depression, and the Pentecostal Church" that mental health issues like depression are still explained in many Pentecostal churches solely by a "demonic or supernatural explanatory model," and not as an illness like others that require a physician's care; cf. Dawn Davis, "Strong Black Women, Depression, and the Pentecostal Church" (PhD diss., Walden University, 2019), 62, https://scholarworks.waldenu.edu/cgi/viewcontent.cgi?article=7829&context=dissertations. Consequently, these supernatural models that are used in Pentecostal churches like COGIC can make going to a mental health provider seem not only nonsensical but like a lack in trust in God's ability to deliver a person who is sick without human agency, even though this is not the denomination's official position. Jessica Y. Brown's argument about mental health conditions in the Black Church is well taken when she says that "if someone has a diagnosable mental health condition, we cannot pray it away, just as we can't pray away a heart attack or diabetes. We pray, and then we seek the help and support we need"; cf. Jessica Y. Brown, "Ministry for Mental Health in the Black Church," The Christian Citizen, April 15, 2020, 2. However, her statement seems to fail to consider how

a large segment of the Black Church—Pentecostals in particular—view sickness and disease from a "paramodern" perspective because of their belief in divine healing in a post-modern age; Kenneth J. Archer, A Pentecostal Hermeneutic Spirit, Scripture, and Community (Cleveland: CPTI Press, 2009), 45. This paramodern classification of Pentecostalism, of which COGIC is a part, acknowledges that Pentecostalism emerged in the modern era (early twentieth century) and as such is not against modernity and science (cf. Ibid., 44). Nevertheless, Pentecostalism rejects the notion that has come to define most of what being scientific and modern has come to mean, and that is that God does not act in this age supernaturally through miracles or heal sickness and disease in this age without human assistance (cf. Ibid., 39, 43-45). Consequently, one of the articles of COGIC's statement of faith says, "We believe that the redemptive work of Christ on the cross provides healing for the human body in answering a believing prayer" (cf. https://www.cogic.org/about-us/statement-of-faith/). Thus, the term "paramodern," used to describe Pentecostalism, signifies that the tradition in some ways still exists "upon the fridges of modernity" (cf. Ibid., 45). Consequently, it is not the case that Pentecostals do not believe that mental illness is an illness like any other illness such as heart disease or cancer. On the contrary, the real problem is that Pentecostals' paramodern belief in divine healing sometimes gets in the way of its members getting the treatment that they need because seeking such treatment is thought by some in the tradition to be a lack of faith; cf. Davis, "Strong Black Women," 62.

[4] Dawn Davis notes that some clergy did not refer their members to clinicians to treat depression because they did not know how to "locate mental health professionals who were competent and trustworthy to provide culturally sensitive service" (cf. Ibid., 59-60).

[5] Dawn Davis notes that some clergy did not refer their members to clinicians to treat depression because they did not know how to "locate mental health professionals who were competent and trustworthy to

provide culturally sensitive service" (cf. Ibid.).

[6] Haugk, *Antagonist in the Church*, 27.

[7] Ibid., 29.

[8] Brown, "Ministry for Mental Health," 2.

[9] Darrell Puls gives an example of this when he writes about narcissist personality disorder (NPD) among pastors. He said, "There is good reason to believe that the pastorate is attractive to 'religious' narcissists. There is no other profession where one gets to stand in front of people every week and tell them as an expert and on God's behalf how they are to live, how their sins and shortcomings are getting in their way, and then be told over and over afterwards what a wonderful message he or she just delivered. Pastors are automatically invited into every nook and cranny of human existence, from weddings to tragic death, and are told our deepest, darkest secrets along with our aspirations for the future, are sought out for advice and then invited to dinner as knowledge about other people, this is it. The problem is how pastors with dangerously high levels of narcissism use it to control, manipulate, exploit, and abuse those around them"; cf. Darrell Puls, *Let Us Prey: The Plague of Narcissist Pastors and What We Can Do about It* Revised Edition (Eugene: Cascade Books, 2020), iii.

[10] Agabi Ayuba, "The Effects of Dementia in the Life of a Pastor," a seminar paper in partial fulfillment for the ACPE at Nigerian Baptist Theological Seminary Ogbomoso, March 2021, 4, https://www.academia.edu/45523493/_Effects_of_Dementia_in_the_Life_of_a_Pastor.

[11] Ibid., 10.

[12] COGIC does not use mental or physical incapacitations as a charge or grounds to remove a pastor from a local congregation; cf. C. F. Range Jr., ed., Church of God in Christ Official Manual (Memphis: Church of God in Christ Publishing House, 1973), 31. This constitutional problem

can be resolved if the COGIC General Assembly completes a long-overdue revision of the denomination's constitution.

[13]. A "prayer warrior" is a term used in the Holiness-Pentecostal Tradition. Prayer warriors are known to be given to frequent prayer, and their prayer ministries have a reputation for generating positive results, such as—but not limited to—numerous conversions, Spirit baptisms, physical healings, etc. COGIC evangelist such as Mothers E. J. Dabney and Elsie Shaw were examples of those who were known as a "prayer warrior," who had "the spirit of prayer, like unto his [Bishop Charles H. Mason] ministry"; E. J. Dabney, What It Means to Pray Through (Memphis: COGIC Bookstore Distributors, 1987), 36. This emphasis on the primacy of prayer is an example of the "black slave tradition" that Bishop C. H. Mason sought to preserve institutionally within the denomination he founded, and what he saw in open display in the famous Azusa Street Revival of 1906 under Elder William J. Seymour; cf. Ithiel C. Clemmons, Bishop C. H. Mason and the Roots of the Church of God in Christ (Bakersfield: Pneuma Life Publishing, 1996), 22, 31-33.

[14] It is interesting that prayer warriors are seen as being in ministry regardless of whether they are ordained as elders. Although we have examples of ordained elders, such as Bishop C. H. Mason, who are prayer warriors, most prayer warriors are not ordained and are overwhelmingly female; cf. Dabney, What It Means to Pray Through, 33, 36. This gives these women enormous spiritual authority over the male clergy even though they are submitted to them in the denominational polity, as they are seen as bearers of spiritual power birthed out of their lives of prayer and consecration.

[15] Accessed January 10, 2018, https://gardenofprayercogic.org/.

[16] Ibid., 33.

[17] Ibid., 16.

[18] Ibid.

[19] Ibid., 51.

[20] Ibid., 51-52.

[21] Elton H. Weaver III, *Bishop Charles H. Mason in the Age of Jim Crow: The Struggle for Religious and Moral Uplift* (Lanham: The Rowman and Littlefield Publishing Group, Inc., 2020), 10.

[22] Otha M. Kelly, *Profile of a Churchman: The Life of Otha M. Kelly in the Church of God in Christ* (Jamaica: K and C Publishers, Inc., 1976), 112-13.

[23] Ibid., 74.

[24] Ibid., 75-76.

[25.] Ibid., 76.

[26] Ibid., 74.

[27] Ibid., 36, 74.

[28] Ibid., 33, 79.

[29] Bobby Bean, *This Is the Church of God in Christ* (Atlanta: Underground Epics Publishing, 2001), 91. Other documented cases exist where Bishop Mason used prayer as a conflict resolution tool in the General Assembly of the denomination recorded in the official minutes of the denomination on December 7, 1948. It said, "Bishop Williams the National Chairman now presiding; Elder Shipman moved that the Chair appoint a committee to approach Bishop Mason on this subject. The motion was seconded by Elder Cole. The Chair then appointed the following committeemen, Bishop O. T. Jones, Bishop A. B. McEwen, and Elder L. C. Patrick. At this time, Bishop Mason came, and the council suspended all business. Bishop Mason prayed that God rebuke the evil and work wonders in the minds of the ministers. After prayer he sat and taught the ministers as a father would teach his children. He sang in the spirit until all rejoiced in the Lord. He then emphasized the need of unity and godliness among us. He further stated that, the brother than sins is to be rebuked, and when

he repents he is to be forgiven, that repentance brings forgiveness"; cf. A. Z. Hall, ed., *Church of God in Christ Minutes of the General Assembly of the Church of God in Christ, Inc.* (Memphis: COGIC Publishing Board, 7 December 1948), X.

[30] Dabney, *What It Means to Pray Through*, 35.

[31] Ibid., 36; information about Bishop Samuel Kelsey can be found in this article from the *Washington Post* that marked his death; cf. https://www.washingtonpost.com/archive/local/1993/01/15/bishop-samuel-kelsey-broadcast-pastor-dies/18401047-dc58-4a70-a853-23538bc571e6/.

[32.] Ibid., 61.

[33] Ibid.

[34] Ibid., 21.

[35] Ibid.

[36] It is significant that those given in the spirit of prayer are talked about in military terms as those who are "God's warrior on the battlefield," who fight through prayer "to defeat the devil and claim the victory" (Dabney, *What It Means to Pray Through*, 28, 66, 68).

[37] William H. Willimon, *Preaching about Conflict in the Local Church* (Philadelphia: The Westminster Press, 1987), 27.

[38] Ibid.

[39] Alphonetta Wines, "Preaching through Conflict," in *The Working Preacher from Luther Seminary*, April 8, 2016, https://www.workingpreacher.org/sermon-development/preaching-through-congregational-conflict.

[40] James Forbes, *The Holy Spirit and Preaching* (Nashville: Abingdon Press, 1989), 56.

[41] Ibid., 60.

[42] Although COGIC recognizes that "thousands of talented, Spirit-filled, dedicated and well-informed devout women" are useful to the work of the ministry as teachers and preachers who proclaim the gospel, they do not ordain them, as the denomination does not believe that it is Scriptural to have women as elders and bishops; cf. Range Jr., *Church of God Official Manual*, 144-46. Bishop Mason created a system of denominational polity that allowed him and the male leadership that followed him to "view roles and structures of the patriarchy in a new way" based on Mason's expanded view of the women's ministry, which he gained from the Azusa Street Revival; cf. Raynard Smith, ed., "The Church of God in Christ Transforms Women's Ministries through the Positive Influence of Chief Apostle Bishop C. H. Mason," in *With Signs Following: The Life and Ministry of Charles Harrison Mason* (St. Louis: Christian Board Publishers, 2015), 95. Bishop Mason's innovative system in the Black Church was to permit women to have "a degree of empowerment" by working alongside men in ministry, which was unique compared with what existed in other denominations of his day. At the same time, men were still to maintain "strategic ecclesial authority" by keeping the women subject to the male leadership (e.g., pastor, district superintendent, bishop) (cf. Ibid., 82). In so doing, COGIC congregations mirrored a family where the pastor, or the spiritual father, was the head of the house, and the church mother—who was often the evangelist in the local church—functioned like "a wife is to her husband in the home"; cf. Anthea D. Butler, *Women in the Church of God in Christ: Making a Sanctified World* (Chapel Hill: The University of North Carolina Press, 2007), 48-49.

[43] Butler, *Women in the Church of God in Christ*, 53.

CHAPTER FIVE

LOOKING FORWARD, LOOKING BACK

"Don't stop praying, the Lord is nigh
Don't stop praying, he'll hear your cry.
The Lord has promised, and his word is true,
Don't stop praying, he'll answer you."

This book began by looking at two of the many unfortunate examples of past congregational conflicts within the Church of God in Christ, Inc. that spilled out into the media spotlight. The reason for highlighting these two cases of destructive church conflicts was to show that crafting an effective solution to combat and resolve church disputes within COGIC was not merely a lofty, abstract ecclesiastical endeavor but an existential necessity for the peace and well-being of the denomination.

This book aimed to provide a tool that would confront, manage, and effectively resolve destructive congregational disputes within COGIC that are informed by research, biblical in their basis, and rooted in the theological tradition of the largest Pentecostal denomination in North America with a presence in over 100 countries around the world. This project has asserted that a COGIC conflict resolution team is the best approach in dealing with the menace of destructive church disputes that tear the fabric of congregational bonds for three reasons. First, the spiritual and emotional strain of church conflicts can swiftly overwhelm clergy and laity individuals. A COGIC conflict resolution team can confront the spiritual and psychological onslaught of a church conflict in the unity of a quorum of anointed, prayerful, and gifted persons instead of one person facing a church crisis alone. Second, a COGIC conflict resolution team is the best approach to dealing with church conflict because it is closely aligned with the total datum of Scripture. Surprisingly, our research has revealed that the communal approach to church conflict is advocated more in the biblical text than individual ones. Third, a COGIC conflict resolution team can harness the resources of its jurisdiction to confront a church conflict as opposed to a local church or pastor dealing with the problems of destructive church discord alone.

This innovative tool supported by this book can be a vital resource for COGIC pastors and churches within the denomination, and it will augment the benefit of COGIC affiliation in an age when congregations and pastors question the relevance of belonging to any ecclesiastical connectional body.

The contents of our research have shown that a COGIC conflict resolution team would have a twofold benefit. On the one hand, this proposed conflict resolution tool would benefit the COGIC because it would be innovative, as we have shown. After all, no official denominational approach exists to prevent, combat, and resolve church disputes. Conversely, COGIC would benefit from a denominationally sanctioned conflict resolution team because it would bring a quorum of persons of varied but complementary skill sets and gifts of both genders to deal with destructive congregational conflict.

One fundamental limitation of this study is that this model has not been tested as it has been presented in this dissertation. Unfortunately, the author was not able to test this model in a COGIC congregation because he does not currently serve in a pastoral charge. Also, the author was limited in testing this project because he has been forward deployed overseas, preventing him from presenting this model to COGIC jurisdictional bishops that he may use in a congregation gripped by a conflict under their charge. Nevertheless, the General Assembly of COGIC should strongly consider adopting this model despite the limitation because the author is confident that when it is tested, it will prove to be fruitful in assisting the saints to walk together and not get weary.

BIBLIOGRAPHY

Ammerman, Nancy T. et al. *Studying Congregation: A New Handbook.* Nashville: Abingdon Press, 1998.

Anyabwile, Thabiti, and Isaac Adams. "The Difference between a Healthy and Peaceful Church." *The Front Porch,* January 9, 2016. https://thefrontporch.org/2016/02/the-difference-between-a-healthy-and-a-peaceful-church/.

Archer, Kenneth J. *A Pentecostal Hermeneutic Spirit, Scripture, and Community.* Cleveland: CPTI Press, 2009.

Ayuba, Agabi. "The Effects of Dementia in the Life of a Pastor." A seminar paper in partial fulfillment for the ACPE at Nigerian Baptist Theological Seminary Ogbomoso, March 2021, 4. https://www.academia.edu/45523493/_Effects_of_Dementia_in_the_Life_of_a_Pastor.

Baldwin, James. "Down at the Cross." In *James Baldwin: Collected Essays,* edited by Tony Morrison New York: Penguin Random House, 1998.

Bean, Bobby. *This Is the Church of God in Christ.* Atlanta: Underground Epics Publishing, 2001.

Bixby, Doug. *Navigating the Nonsense: Church Conflict and Triangulation.* Eugene: Cascade Books, 2016.

Blomberg, Craig S. *The New American Commentary: An Exegetical and Theological Exposition of Holy Scripture Matthew,* vol. 22. Nashville: B and H Publishing Company, 1992.

Bolman, Lee G., and Terrence E. Deal. *Reframing Organizations: Artistry, Choice, and Leadership.* San Francisco: John Wiley and Sons, Inc., 2003.

Brown, Jessica Y. "Ministry for Mental Health in the Black Church." *The Christian Citizen,* April 15, 2020.

Burnaby, John, ed. "The Spirit and the Letter." In *Augustine: Later Works,* 182-195. Philadelphia: The Westminster Press, 1955.

Burns, Bob, Tasha D. Chapman, and Donald C. Guthrie. *The Politics of Ministry: Navigating Power Dynamics and Negotiating Interest.* Downers Grove: InterVarsity Press, 2019.

Butler, Anthea D. *Women in the Church of God in Christ: Making a Sanctified World.* Chapel Hill: The University of North Carolina Press, 2007.

Clemmons, Ithiel C. *Bishop C. H. Mason and the Roots of the Church of God in Christ.* Bakersfield: Pneuma Life Publishing, 1996.

COGIC Abuse Watch. "Numerous Assault Complaints Filed against National Trustee Cari Barnes." July 3, 2014. https://cogicabusewatch.wordpress.com/tag/williams-temple/.

Culpepper, R. Alan. *Matthew: A Commentary.* Louisville: Westminster John Knox Press, 2021.

Dabney, E. J. *What It Means to Pray Through.* Memphis: COGIC Bookstore Distributors, 1987.

Davis, Dawn. "Strong Black Women, Depression, and the Pentecostal Church." PhD diss., Walden University, 2019. https://scholarworks.waldenu.edu/cgi/viewcontent.cgi?article=7829&context=dissertations.

Delitzsch, C. F., and F. Keil. *Commentary on the Old Testament Volumes 6 Proverbs, Ecclesiastes, Song of Solomon.* Peabody: Hendrickson Publishers, Inc., 1966.
Dunn, James D. G. *The Theology of Paul the Apostle.* Grand Rapids: William B. Eerdmans Publishing Company, 1998.

Earls, Aaron. "The Church Growth Gap: The Big Get Bigger and the Small Get Smaller." *Christianity Today*, March 6, 2019. https://www.christianitytoday.com/news/2019/march/lifeway-research-church-growth-attendance-size.html.

Egolf, Donald B., and Sandra L Chester. *Forming, Storming, Norming, Performing: Successful Communication in Groups and Teams*, 3rd ed. Bloomington: Universe, Inc., 2001.

Everist, Norma Cook. *Church Conflict: From Contention to Collaboration.* Nashville: Abingdon Press, 2004.

Firch, James. "Church and Religious Charitable Giving Statistics." Nonprofit Source, 2020. https://nonprofitssource.com/online-giving-statistics/church-giving/.

Florido, Adrian. "Feeling a Different Pulse in the Heart of Black San Diego." *Voice of San Diego,* March 13, 2011. https://www.voiceofsandiego.org/neighborhoods/feeling-a-different-pulse-in-the-heart-of-black-san-diego/.

Forbes, James. *The Holy Spirit and Preaching.* Nashville: Abingdon Press, 1989.

France, R. T. *The New International Commentary on the New Testament: The Gospel of Matthew.* Grand Rapids and Cambridge: William B. Eerdmans Publishing Company, 2007.

Fredrickson, David. "'Through Many Tears' (2 Cor. 2:4): Paul's Grieving

Letter and the Occasion of 2 Corinthians 2:1-7." Luther's Digital Commons Faculty Publications, (2001). https://digitalcommons.luthersem.edu/cgi/viewcontent.cgi?article=1215&context=faculty_articles.

Freedman, David N., ed. *The Anchor Bible Dictionary*, vol. 2 D-G. New York: Double Day, 1992.

Frick, Frank S. *A Journey through the Hebrews Scriptures.* Fort Worth: Harcourt Brace and Company, 1995.

Gangel, Kenneth O., and Samuel L. Canine. *Communication and Conflict Management in Churches and Christian Organizations.* Nashville: Broadman Press, 1992.

Hall, A. Z., ed. *Church of God in Christ Minutes of the General Assembly 1934-1960.* Memphis: Church of God in Christ Publishing House, 2001.

Hare, Michael. *When Church Conflict Happens: A Proven Process for Resolving Unhealthy Disagreements and Embracing Healthy Ones* Chicago: Moody Publishers, 2019.

Haugk, Kenneth. *Antagonist in the Church: How to Identify and Deal with Destructive Conflict.* Minneapolis: Augsburg Publishing House, 1988.

Henderson Jr., Ulesses C., Esq. "Pacific Mount Olive Chronology of Events." Office of the General Council of the Church of God in Christ, Inc., November 11, 2016. http://cogicjustice.net/wp-content/uploads/2016/11/2016-11-03-Statement-on-Mount-Olive-COGIC.pdf.

Jones, Charles Price. "I Will Make the Darkness Light." In *Yes Lord! Church of God in Christ Hymnal*, Memphis: Church of God in Christ Publishing Board, 1982.

Keener, Craig S. *A Commentary on the Gospel of Matthew.* Grand Rapids and Cambridge: William B. Eerdmans Publishing Company, 1999.

Kelley, Geffrey B., ed. *Life Together.* Minneapolis: Fortress Press, 1996.

Kelly, Otha M. *Profile of a Churchman: The Life of Otha M. Kelly in the Church of God in Christ.* Jamaica: K and C Publishers, Inc., 1976.

Lacy Individually Represented as Williams Temple Church of God in Christ Court of Appeals Texas, Fourteenth District, Houston. March 30, 2004.

Lauzurek, Michelle. "When the Pastor You Love Leaves Your Church." *Crosswalk*, November 19, 2018. https://www.crosswalk.com/church/pastors-or-leadership/when-the-pastor-you-love-leaves-your-church-10-ways-to-navigate-pastoral-transition.html.

Levy, Claudia. "Bishop Samuel Kelsey, Broadcast Pastor, Dies." *Washington Post*, January 15, 1993. https://www.washingtonpost.com/archive/local/1993/01/15/bishop-samuel-kelsey-broadcast-pastor-dies/18401047-dc58-4a70-a853-23538bc571e6/.

Lull, Timothy F., ed. "Bondage of the Will." In *Martin Luther's Basic Theological Writings,* 173-223. Minneapolis: Fortress Press, 1989.

Malphurs, Aubrey. *Look Before You Lead: How to Discern and Shape Your Church Culture.* Grand Rapids: Baker Books, 2013.

McNeill, John T., ed. *Calvin Christian Institutes of Religion Book II.* Philadelphia: The Westminster Press, 1960.

Meilick Jr., Richard R. *The New American Commentary: An Exegetical and Theological Exposition of Holy Scripture Philippians, Colossians, Philemon,* vol. 32. Nashville: B and H Publishing Group, 1991.

Monroe, Laundale. "Family Systems in Congregational Settings." *Ministry: International Journal for Pastors,* June 2009. https://www.ministrymagazine.org/archive/2009/06/family-systems.

Morrison, Tony, ed. *James Baldwin: Collected Essays.* New York: Penguin Random House, 1998.

Murphy-O'Conner, Jerome. *Paul the Letter-Writer: His World, His Options, His Skill.* Collegeville: The Liturgical Press.

Nolan, Bruce. "Pentecostal Bishop Charles Brown Booked With Sexual Battery." *The Times-Picayune,* September 21, 2011. https://www.nola.com/news/crime_police/article_0242250c-fff9-5d6b-a5b1-d6d3f1c5e0a4.html

________. "COGIC Reinstates Bishop after Criminal Case Is Dropped." *The Washington Post,* March 7, 2012. https://www.washingtonpost.com/national/on-faith/cogic-reinstates-bishop-after-criminal-charges-dropped/2012/03/07/gIQAjUfGxR_story.html.

Poirier, Alfred. *The Peace-Making Pastor: A Biblical Guide to Resolving Church Conflict.* Grand Rapids: Baker Books, 2006.

Puls, Darrell. *Let Us Prey: The Plague of Narcissist Pastors and What We Can Do about It,* Revised Edition. Eugene: Cascade Books, 2020.

Range Jr., C. F., ed. *Church of God in Christ Official Manual.* Memphis: Church of God in Christ Publishing House, 1973.

Sandstrom, Alexander. "Church Involvement Varies Widely among US Christians." Pew Research Group, last modified November 16, 2015. https://www.pewresearch.org/fact-tank/2015/11/16/church-involvement-varies-widely-among-u-s-christians/.

Simerson, John. "Sex Charge against a Pentecostal Bishop Was Filed

Too Late, Judge Says." *The Times-Picayune,* March 3, 2012. https://www.nola.com/news/crime_police/article_40aed0ae-4e4a-5737-bf93-62474a569dd1.html.

Sisson, Carmen K. "Why African-Americans Are Moving Back to the South." *The Christian Science Monitor,* March 16, 2014. https://www.csmonitor.com/USA/Society/2014/0316/Why-African-Americans-are-moving-back-to-the-South.

Smith, Raynard, ed. *With Signs Following: The Life and Ministry of Charles Harrison Mason.* St. Louis: Christian Board Publishers, 2015.

Steinke, Peter L. *Healthy Congregations: A Systems Approach.* Lanham: Rowman and Litchfield, 1996.

Thayer, John H. *Thayer's Greek-English Lexicon of the New Testament.* Grand Rapids: Baker Books, 1977.

Vanderbloen, William. "How to Deal with the Unexpected Loss of a Pastor." July 1, 2017. https://www.vanderbloemen.com/blog/unexpected-loss-pastor.

Weaver III, Elton H. *Bishop Charles H. Mason in the Age of Jim Crow: The Struggle for Religious and Moral Uplift.* Lanham: Lexington Books, 2020.

Wesley, Charles. "A Charge I Have to Keep." In *Yes Lord! Church of God in Christ Hymnal,* Memphis: The Church of God in Christ Publishing Board, 1982.

Whacker, Grant. *Heaven Below: Early Pentecostals and American Culture.* Cambridge: Harvard University Press, 2001.

Willimon, William H. *Preaching about Conflict in the Local Church.* Philadelphia: The Westminster Press, 1987.

Wines, Alphonetta. "Preaching through Conflict." In *The Working Preacher from Luther Seminary,* April 8, 2016, https://www.workingpreacher.org/sermon-development/preaching-through-congregational-conflict.

Zizioulas, John D. *Being as Communion: Studies in Personhood and the Church.* Crestwood: St. Vladimir's Seminary Press, 1985.

Garden of Prayer Church of God in Christ https://gardenofprayercogic.org/.